NINJA FOODI
SMART XL GRILL
COOKBOOK

*Delicious, simple, and quick recipes to enjoy daily
with your Ninja Foodi Smart XL Grill.
Grill inside without losing the true taste of the outside grill.*

ELIZABETH A. HARRIS

⏰ Prep Time 15 m | ⏰ Cooking Time 20 m | 4 Servings

Ingredients:

- 1 short crust pastry
- ½ cup leftover macaroni n' cheese
- 2 tablespoons plain Greek yogurt
- 1 teaspoon garlic puree
- 11 ounces milk
- 2 large eggs
- 2 tablespoons Parmesan cheese, grated

Instructions:

1. Dust 4 ramekins with a little flour.
2. Line the bottom of prepared ramekins with short crust pastry.
3. In a bowl, mix together macaroni, yogurt and garlic.
4. Transfer the macaroni mixture between ramekins about ¾ full.
5. In a small bowl, add the milk and eggs and beat well.
6. Place the egg mixture over the macaroni mixture and top with the cheese evenly.
7. Arrange the "Crisper Basket" in the pot of Ninja Foodi Grill.
8. Close the Ninja Foodi Grill with lid and select "Air Crisp".
9. Set the temperature to 355 degrees F to preheat.
10. Press "Start/Stop" to begin preheating.
11. When the display shows "Add Food" open the lid and place the ramekin into the "Crisper Basket".
12. Close the Ninja Foodi Grill with lid and set the time for 20 minutes.
13. Press "Start/Stop" to begin cooking.
14. When the cooking time is completed, press "Start/Stop" to stop cooking and open the lid.
15. Serve hot.

Nutritional Information per Serving:

Calories: 209 | Fat: 10.4g | Saturated Fat: 2.9g | Carbohydrates: 19.1g | Sugar: 4.6g | Protein: 9.6g

⏰ Prep Time 15 m | ⏲ Cooking Time 12 m | 2 Servings

Ingredients:

- ½ of frozen ready-made pie crust
- ¼ tablespoon olive oil
- 1 small egg
- 3 tablespoons cheddar cheese, grated
- 1½ tablespoons whipping cream
- Salt and freshly ground black pepper, to taste
- 3 tablespoons boiled broccoli, chopped
- 2 tablespoons cooked chicken, chopped

Instructions:

1. Cut 1 (5-inch) round from the pie crust.
2. Arrange the pie crust round in a small pie pan and gently press in the bottom and sides.
3. In a bowl, mix together the egg, cheese, cream, salt, and black pepper.
4. Pour the egg mixture over dough base and top with the broccoli and chicken.
5. Arrange the "Crisper Basket" in the pot of Ninja Foodi Grill.
6. Close the Ninja Foodi Grill with lid and select "Air Crisp".
7. Set the temperature to 390 degrees F to preheat.
8. Press "Start/Stop" to begin preheating.
9. When the display shows "Add Food" open the lid and place the pan into the "Crisper Basket".
10. Close the Ninja Foodi Grill with lid and set the time for 12 minutes.
11. Press "Start/Stop" to begin cooking.
12. When cooking time is completed, press "Start/Stop" to stop cooking and open the lid.
13. Cut into equal-sized wedges and serve.

Nutritional Information per Serving:

Calories: 197 | Fat: 15g | Saturated Fat: 5.9g | Carbohydrates: 7.4g | Sugar: 0.9g | Protein: 8.6g

⏰ Prep Time 15 m | ⏰ Cooking Time 20 m | 2 Servings

Ingredients:

- 5½ ounces salmon fillet, chopped
- Salt and freshly ground black pepper, to taste
- ½ tablespoon fresh lemon juice
- 1 egg yolk
- 3½ tablespoons chilled butter
- 2/3 cup flour
- 1 tablespoon cold water
- 2 eggs
- 3 tablespoons whipping cream
- 1 scallion, chopped

Instructions:

1. In a bowl, mix together the salmon, salt, black pepper and lemon juice.
2. In another bowl, add the egg yolk, butter, flour and water and mix until a dough forms.
3. Place the dough onto a floured smooth surface and roll into about 7-inch round.
4. Place the dough in a quiche pan and press firmly in the bottom and along the edges.
5. Trim the excess edges.
6. In a small bowl, add the eggs, cream, salt and black pepper and beat until well combined.
7. Place the cream mixture over crust evenly and top with the salmon mixture, followed by the scallion.
8. Arrange the "Crisper Basket" in the pot of Ninja Foodi Grill.
9. Close the Ninja Foodi Grill with lid and select "Air Crisp".
10. Set the temperature to 355 degrees F to preheat.
11. Press "Start/Stop" to begin preheating.
12. When the display shows "Add Food" open the lid and place the pan into the "Crisper Basket".
13. Close the Ninja Foodi Grill with lid and set the time for 20 minutes.
14. Press "Start/Stop" to begin cooking.
15. When cooking time is completed, press "Start/Stop" to stop cooking and open the lid.
16. Cut into equal-sized wedges and serve.

Nutritional Information per Serving:

Calories: 592 | Fat: 39g | Saturated Fat: 20.1g | Carbohydrates: 33.8g | Sugar: 0.8g | Protein: 27.2g

⏰ Prep Time 15 m | ⏰ Cooking Time 20 m | 6 Servings

Ingredients:

- 1 teaspoon olive oil
- 1 pound ground sausage
- 1 green bell pepper, seeded and chopped
- ¼ cup onion, chopped
- 8 eggs, beaten
- ½ cup Colby Jack cheese, shredded
- 1 teaspoon fennel seed
- ½ teaspoon garlic salt

Instructions:

1. In a skillet, heat the oil over medium heat and cook the sausage for about 4-5 minutes.
2. Add the bell pepper and onion and cook for about 4-5 minutes
3. Remove from the heat and transfer the sausage mixture into a bowl to cool slightly.
4. In a baking pan, place the sausage mixture and top with the cheese, followed by the beaten eggs, fennel seed and garlic salt.
5. Arrange the "Crisper Basket" in the pot of Ninja Foodi Grill.
6. Close the Ninja Foodi Grill with lid and select "Air Crisp".
7. Set the temperature to 390 degrees F to preheat.
8. Press "Start/Stop" to begin preheating.
9. When the display shows "Add Food" open the lid and place the pan into the "Crisper Basket".
10. Close the Ninja Foodi Grill with lid and set the time for 15 minutes.
11. Press "Start/Stop" to begin cooking.
12. When cooking time is completed, press "Start/Stop" to stop cooking and open the lid.
13. Cut into equal-sized wedges and serve.

Nutritional Information per Serving:

Calories: 394 | Fat: 1.1g | Saturated Fat: 10.8g | Carbohydrates: 3.1g | Sugar: 1.7g | Protein: 24.4g

⏰ Prep Time 15 m | ⏰ Cooking Time 35 m | 5 Servings

Ingredients:

- 1½ tablespoons olive oil
- ½ of large onion, chopped
- 24 ounces frozen Hashbrown
- 3 eggs

- 2 tablespoons milk
- Salt and freshly ground black pepper, to taste
- ½ ounces ham, chopped
- ¼ cup Cheddar cheese, shredded

Instructions:

1. In a skillet, heat the oil over medium heat and sauté the onion for about 4-5 minutes.
2. Remove from the heat and transfer the onion into a bowl.
3. Add the Hashbrown and mix well.
4. Place the mixture into a baking pan.
5. Arrange the "Crisper Basket" in the pot of Ninja Foodi Grill.
6. Close the Ninja Foodi Grill with lid and select "Bake".
7. Set the temperature to 350 degrees F to preheat.
8. Press "Start/Stop" to begin preheating.
9. When the display shows "Add Food" open the lid and place the pan into the "Crisper Basket".
10. Close the Ninja Foodi Grill with lid and set the time for 32 minutes.
11. Press "Start/Stop" to begin cooking.
12. Stir the mixture once after 8 minutes.
13. Meanwhile, in a bowl, add the eggs, milk, salt and black pepper and beat well.
14. After 15 minutes of cooking, place the egg mixture over Hashbrown mixture evenly and top with the ham.
15. After 30 minutes of cooking, sprinkle the casserole with the cheese.
16. When cooking time is completed, press "Start/Stop" to stop cooking and open the lid.
17. Cut into equal-sized wedges and serve.

Nutritional Information per Serving:

Calories: 540 | Fat: 29.8g | Saturated Fat: 6.5g | Carbohydrates: 51.5g | Sugar: 3.2g | Protein: 16.7g

⏰ Prep Time 10 m | ⏰ Cooking Time 13 m | 2 Servings

Ingredients:

- 2 teaspoons unsalted butter, softened
- 2 ounces cooked chicken, chopped
- 4 large eggs, divided
- Salt and freshly ground black pepper, to taste
- 2 tablespoons heavy cream
- 1/8 teaspoon smoked paprika
- 3 tablespoons Parmesan cheese, grated finely
- 2 teaspoons fresh parsley, minced

Instructions:

1. Arrange the "Crisper Basket" in the pot of Ninja Foodi Grill.
2. Close the Ninja Foodi Grill with lid and select "Air Crisp".
3. Set the temperature to 320 degrees F to preheat.
4. Press "Start/Stop" to begin preheating.
5. In the bottom of a baking pan, spread butter.
6. Arrange the chicken pieces over the butter.
7. In a bowl, add 1 egg, salt, black pepper and cream and beat until smooth.
8. Place the egg mixture over the chicken pieces evenly.
9. Carefully crack the remaining eggs on top and sprinkle with paprika, salt, black pepper, cheese and parsley evenly.
10. When the display shows "Add Food" open the lid and place the pan into the "Crisper Basket".
11. Close the Ninja Foodi Grill with lid and set the time for 13 minutes.
12. Press "Start/Stop" to begin cooking.
13. When the cooking time is completed, press "Start/Stop" to stop cooking and open the lid.
14. Cut into equal-sized wedges and serve.

Nutritional Information per Serving:

Calories: 199 | Fat: 14.7g | Saturated Fat: 6.7g | Carbohydrates: 0.8g | Sugar: 0.5g | Protein: 16.1g

⏰ Prep Time 15 m | ⏰ Cooking Time 10 m | 2 Servings

Ingredients:

- 6 small button mushroom, quartered
- 6 cherry tomatoes, halved
- 4 shaved ham slices
- 2 tablespoons salad greens
- 1 cup cheddar cheese, shredded
- 2 eggs
- 1 tablespoon fresh rosemary, chopped
- Salt and freshly ground black pepper, to taste

Instructions:

1. In a bowl, add the mushrooms, tomatoes, ham and greens.
2. Place half of the vegetable mixture in a greased baking pan.
3. Top with half of the cheese.
4. Repeat the layers once.
5. Make 2 wells in the mixture and carefully crack the eggs in the wells.
6. Sprinkle with rosemary, salt and black pepper.
7. Arrange the "Crisper Basket" in the pot of Ninja Foodi Grill.
8. Close the Ninja Foodi Grill with lid and select "Air Crisp".
9. Set the temperature to 320 degrees to preheat.
10. Press "Start/Stop" to begin preheating.
11. When the display shows "Add Food" open the lid and place the pan into the "Crisper Basket".
12. Close the Ninja Foodi Grill with lid and set the time for 10 minutes.
13. Press "Start/Stop" to begin cooking.
14. When the cooking time is completed, press "Start/Stop" to stop cooking and open the lid.
15. Cut into equal-sized wedges and serve.

Nutritional Information per Serving:

Calories: 480 | Fat: 30.3g | Saturated Fat: 15.1g | Carbohydrates: 20.4g | Sugar: 11.3g | Protein: 33.9g

⏰ Prep Time 10 m | ⏰ Cooking Time 12 m | 2 Servings

Ingredients:

- ¼ cup oats
- ¼ cup refined flour
- ½ teaspoon baking powder
- ¼ cup powdered sugar
- ¼ cup unsalted butter, softened
- ¼ cup banana, peeled and mashed
- 1 teaspoon milk
- 1 tablespoon walnuts, chopped

Instructions:

1. In a bowl, mix together the oats, flour and baking powder.
2. In another bowl, add the sugar and butter and beat until creamy.
3. Add the banana and vanilla extract and beat until well combined.
4. Add the flour mixture and milk in banana mixture and mix until just combined.
5. Fold in the walnuts.
6. Grease 4 muffin moulds.
7. Place the mixture into the prepared muffin molds evenly.
8. Arrange the "Crisper Basket" in the pot of Ninja Foodi Grill.
9. Close the Ninja Foodi Grill with lid and select "Air Crisp".
10. Set the temperature to 320 degrees F to preheat.
11. Press "Start/Stop" to begin preheating.
12. When the display shows "Add Food" open the lid and place the muffin moulds into the "Crisper Basket".
13. Close the Ninja Foodi Grill with lid and set the time for 12 minutes.
14. Press "Start/Stop" to begin cooking.
15. When the cooking time is completed, press "Start/Stop" to stop cooking and open the lid.
16. Place the muffin molds onto a wire rack to cool for about 10 minutes.
17. Carefully invert the muffins onto the wire rack to completely cool before serving.

Nutritional Information per Serving:

Calories: 401 | Fat: 26.3g | Saturated Fat: 14.9g | Carbohydrates: 39.2g | Sugar: 17.3g | Protein: 4.4g

⏰ Prep Time 15 m | ⏰ Cooking Time 25 m | 6 Servings

Ingredients:

- 1¾ cups plain flour
- 1/3 cup white sugar
- 1½ teaspoons baking powder
- ½ teaspoon ground cinnamon
- ¼ teaspoon ground ginger
- ¼ teaspoon salt
- ¾ cup milk
- 1/3 cup applesauce
- 1 cup apple, cored and chopped

Instructions:

1. In a large bowl, mix together the flour, sugar, baking powder, spices, and salt.
2. Add in the milk and applesauce and beat until just combined.
3. Fold in the chopped apple.
4. Grease 12 muffin moulds.
5. Place the mixture into the prepared muffin molds evenly.
6. Arrange the "Crisper Basket" in the pot of Ninja Foodi Grill.
7. Close the Ninja Foodi Grill with lid and select "Air Crisp".
8. Set the temperature to 390 degrees F to preheat.
9. Press "Start/Stop" to begin preheating.
10. When the display shows "Add Food" open the lid and place the muffin moulds into the "Crisper Basket".
11. Close the Ninja Foodi Grill with lid and set the time for 20-25 minutes.
12. Press "Start/Stop" to begin cooking.
13. When the cooking time is completed, press "Start/Stop" to stop cooking and open the lid.
14. Place the muffin molds onto a wire rack to cool for about 10 minutes.
15. Carefully invert the muffins onto the wire rack to completely cool before serving.

Nutritional Information per Serving:

Calories: 217 | Fat: 1.1g | Saturated Fat: 0.4g | Carbohydrates: 47.9g | Sugar: 17.8g | Protein: 4.9g

⏲ Prep Time 10 m | ⏱ Cooking Time 17 m | 6 Servings

Ingredients:

- 6 eggs
- ½ cup milk
- Salt and freshly ground black pepper, to taste

- 1 cup fresh spinach, chopped
- 4 cooked bacon slices, crumbled

Instructions:

1. In a bowl, add the eggs, milk, salt and black pepper and beat until well combined.
2. Add the spinach and stir to combine.
3. Divide the spinach mixture into 6 greased cups of an egg bite mold evenly.
4. Arrange the "Crisper Basket" in the pot of Ninja Foodi Grill.
5. Close the Ninja Foodi Grill with lid and select "Air Crisp".
6. Set the temperature to 325 degrees F to preheat.
7. Press "Start/Stop" to begin preheating.
8. When the display shows "Add Food" open the lid and place the muffin egg bite mold into the "Crisper Basket".
9. Close the Ninja Foodi Grill with lid and set the time for 17 minutes.
10. Press "Start/Stop" to begin cooking.
11. When the cooking time is completed, press "Start/Stop" to stop cooking and open the lid.
12. Place the muffin molds onto a wire rack to cool for about 5 minutes.
13. Carefully invert the muffins onto a platter and top with bacon pieces
14. Serve warm.

Nutritional Information per Serving:

Calories: 179 | Fat: 12.9g | Saturated Fat: 4.3g | Carbohydrates: 1.8g | Sugar: 1.3g | Protein: 13.5g

⏰ Prep Time 15 m | ⏱ Cooking Time 7 m | 6 Servings

Ingredients:

- 1¼ cup whole-wheat flour
- ¼ cup all-purpose flour
- ½ teaspoon baking powder
- 1/8 teaspoon baking soda
- ½ teaspoon dried parsley, crushed
- ¼ teaspoon salt
- ½ cup yogurt
- 1 teaspoon balsamic vinegar
- 1 tablespoon vegetable oil
- 3 tablespoons cottage cheese, grated
- 1 carrot, peeled and grated
- 2-4 tablespoons water (if needed)
- 7 ounces Parmesan cheese, grated
- ¼ cup walnuts, chopped

Instructions:

1. Grease 6 medium muffin moulds.
2. In a large bowl, mix together the flours, baking powder, baking soda, parsley, and salt.
3. In another large bowl, add the yogurt and vinegar and mix well.
4. Add the oil, cottage cheese and carrot and mix well. (Add some water if needed).
5. Make a well in the center of the yogurt mixture.
6. Slowly, add the flour mixture in the well and mix until well combined.
7. Place the mixture into the prepared muffin molds evenly and top with the Parmesan cheese and walnuts.
8. Arrange the "Crisper Basket" in the pot of Ninja Foodi Grill.
9. Close the Ninja Foodi Grill with lid and select "Air Crisp".
10. Set the temperature to 355 degrees F to preheat.
11. Press "Start/Stop" to begin preheating.
12. When the display shows "Add Food" open the lid and place the muffin molds into the "Crisper Basket".
13. Close the Ninja Foodi Grill with lid and set the time for 7 minutes.
14. Press "Start/Stop" to begin cooking.
15. When the cooking time is completed, press "Start/Stop" to stop cooking and open the lid.
16. Place the muffin molds onto a wire rack for about 10 minutes.
17. Carefully invert the muffins onto the wire rack to cool completely before serving.

Nutritional Information per Serving:

Calories: 222 | Fat: 12.9g | Saturated Fat: 5.7g | Carbohydrates: 12.6g | Sugar: 2g | Protein: 15.2g

⏰ Prep Time 20 m | ⏰ Cooking Time 40 m | 10 Servings

Ingredients:

- 1½ cups warm water, divided
- 1½ teaspoons active dry yeast
- 1 teaspoon sugar
- 3 cups all-purpose flour
- 1 cup plain Greek yogurt
- 2 teaspoons kosher salt

Instructions:

1. Add ½ cup of the warm water, yeast and sugar in the bowl of a stand mixer, fitted with the dough hook attachment and mix well.
2. Set aside for about 5 minutes.
3. Add the flour, yogurt, and salt and mix on medium-low speed until the dough comes together.
4. Then, mix on medium speed for 5 minutes.
5. Place the dough into a bowl.
6. With a plastic wrap, cover the bowl and place in a warm place for about 2-3 hours or until doubled in size.
7. Transfer the dough onto a lightly floured surface and shape into a smooth ball.
8. Place the dough onto a greased parchment paper-lined rack.
9. With a kitchen towel, cover the dough and let rest for 15 minutes.
10. With a very sharp knife, cut a 4x½-inch deep cut down the center of the dough.
11. Arrange the "Crisper Basket" in the pot of Ninja Foodi Grill.
12. Close the Ninja Foodi Grill with lid and select "Roast".
13. Set the temperature to 325 degrees F to preheat.
14. Press "Start/Stop" to begin preheating.
15. When the display shows "Add Food" open the lid and carefully place the dough into the "Crisper Basket".
16. Close the Ninja Foodi Grill with lid and set the time for 40 minutes.
17. Press "Start/Stop" to begin cooking.
18. When the cooking time is completed, press "Start/Stop" to stop cooking and open the lid.
19. Carefully place the bread onto wire rack to cool completely before slicing.
20. Cut the bread into desired-sized slices and serve.

Nutritional Information per Serving:

Calories: 157 | Fat: 0.7g | Saturated Fat: 0.3g | Carbohydrates: 31g | Sugar: 2.2g | Protein: 5.5g

⏰ Prep Time 15 m | ⏰ Cooking Time 30 m | 8 Servings

Ingredients:
For Bread:

- 1 cup all-purpose flour
- ¾ teaspoon baking powder
- ¼ teaspoon baking soda
- 1¼ teaspoons ground cinnamon
- ¼ teaspoon salt
- 1/3 cup vegetable oil
- 1/3 cup sugar
- 1 egg

- 1 teaspoon vanilla extract
- ½ cup zucchini, shredded
- ½ cup apple, cored and shredded
- 5 tablespoons walnuts, chopped

For Topping:

- 1 tablespoon walnuts, chopped
- 2 teaspoons brown sugar
- ¼ teaspoon ground cinnamon

Instructions:

1. For bread: in a bowl, mix together the flour, baking powder, baking soda, cinnamon, and salt.
2. In another large bowl, mix well the oil, sugar, egg, and vanilla extract.
3. Add the flour mixture and mix until just combined
4. Gently fold in the zucchini, apple and walnuts.
5. For the topping: in a small bowl, add all the ingredients and whisk them well.
6. Place the mixture into a lightly greased loaf pan and sprinkle with the topping mixture.
7. Arrange the "Crisper Basket" in the pot of Ninja Foodi Grill.
8. Close the Ninja Foodi Grill with lid and select "Air Crisp".
9. Set the temperature to 325 degrees F to preheat.
10. Press "Start/Stop" to begin preheating.
11. When the display shows "Add Food" open the lid and place the pan into the "Crisper Basket".
12. Close the Ninja Foodi Grill with lid and set the time for 30 minutes.
13. Press "Start/Stop" to begin cooking.
14. When the cooking time is completed, press "Start/Stop" to stop cooking and open the lid.
15. Place the pan onto a wire rack to cool for about 10 minutes.
16. Carefully invert the bread onto wire rack to cool completely before slicing.
17. Cut the bread into desired-sized slices and serve.

Nutritional Information per Serving:

Calories: 225 | Fat: 13.3g | Saturated Fat: 2.2g | Carbohydrates: 24g | Sugar: 10.1g | Protein: 3.9g

⏰ Prep Time 10 m | ⏰ Cooking Time 20 m | 8 Servings

Ingredients:

- 1 1/3 cups flour
- 2/3 cup sugar
- 1 teaspoon baking soda
- 1 teaspoon baking powder
- 1 teaspoon ground cinnamon
- ¼ teaspoon salt
- ½ cup milk
- ½ cup olive oil
- 3 bananas, peeled and sliced

Instructions:

1. In the bowl of a stand mixer, add all the ingredients and mix until well combined.
2. Place the mixture into a greased loaf pan.
3. Arrange the "Crisper Basket" in the pot of Ninja Foodi Grill.
4. Close the Ninja Foodi Grill with lid and select "Air Crisp".
5. Set the temperature to 330 degrees F to preheat.
6. Press "Start/Stop" to begin preheating.
7. When the display shows "Add Food" open the lid and place the loaf pan into the "Crisper Basket".
8. Close the Ninja Foodi Grill with lid and set the time for 20 minutes.
9. Press "Start/Stop" to begin cooking.
10. When the cooking time is completed, press "Start/Stop" to stop cooking and open the lid.
11. Place the pan onto a wire rack for about 10 minutes.
12. Carefully invert the bread onto the wire rack to cool completely before slicing.
13. Cut the bread into desired sized slices and serve.

Nutritional Information per Serving:

Calories: 295 | Fat: 13.3g | Saturated Fat: 2.1g | Carbohydrates: 44g | Sugar: 22.8g | Protein: 3.1g

⏰ Prep Time 10 m | ⏰ Cooking Time 25 m | 4 Servings

Ingredients:

- ¼ cup coconut flour
- 2 tablespoons stevia blend
- 1 teaspoon baking powder
- ¾ teaspoon pumpkin pie spice
- ¼ teaspoon ground cinnamon
- 1/8 teaspoon salt
- ¼ cup canned pumpkin
- 2 large eggs
- 2 tablespoons unsweetened almond milk
- 1 teaspoon vanilla extract

Instructions:

1. In a bowl, add the flour, stevia blend, baking powder, spices and salt and mix well.
2. In another large bowl, add the pumpkin, eggs, almond milk, and vanilla extract. Beat until well combined.
3. Add the flour mixture and mix until just combined.
4. Arrange the "Crisper Basket" in the pot of Ninja Foodi Grill.
5. Close the Ninja Foodi Grill with lid and select "Air Crisp".
6. Set the temperature to 350 degrees F to preheat.
7. Press "Start/Stop" to begin preheating.
8. Place the mixture into a greased parchment paper-lined cake pan evenly.
9. When the display shows "Add Food" open the lid and place the pan into the "Crisper Basket".
10. Close the Ninja Foodi Grill with lid and set the time for 25 minutes.
11. Press "Start/Stop" to begin cooking.
12. When the cooking time is completed, press "Start/Stop" to stop cooking and open the lid.
13. Place the bread pan onto a wire rack for about 10 minutes.
14. Carefully remove the bread from pan and place onto a wire rack to cool completely before slicing.
15. Cut the bread into desired-sized slices and serve.

Nutritional Information per Serving:

Calories: 78 | Fat: 3.4g | Saturated Fat: 1.3g | Carbohydrates: 7.5g | Sugar: 0.9g | Protein: 4.4g

⏰ Prep Time 10 m | ⏰ Cooking Time 22 m | 4 Servings

Ingredients:

- 4 (8-ounce) frozen boneless, skinless chicken breasts
- 2 tablespoons olive oil, divided
- Salt and freshly ground black pepper, to taste
- 1 cup BBQ sauce

Instructions:

1. Brush the chicken breasts with ½ tablespoon of oil evenly and season with salt and black pepper.
2. Arrange the "Grill Grate" in the pot of Ninja Foodi Grill.
3. Close the Ninja Foodi Grill with lid and select "Grill" to "Medium" to preheat.
4. Press "Start/Stop" to begin preheating.
5. When the display shows "Add Food" open the lid and place the chicken breasts onto the "Grill Grate".
6. With your hands, gently press down the chicken breasts.
7. Close the Ninja Foodi Grill with lid and set the time for 22 minutes.
8. Press "Start/Stop" to begin cooking.
9. After 10 minutes of cooking, flip the chicken breasts.
10. After 15 minutes of cooking, flip the chicken breasts and coat the upper side with barbecue sauce generously.
11. After 20 minutes of cooking, flip the chicken breasts and coat the upper side with barbecue sauce generously.
12. When the cooking time is completed, press "Start/Stop" to stop cooking and open the lid.
13. Place the chicken breasts onto a platter and set aside for about 5 minutes before serving.

Nutritional Information per Serving:

Calories: 585 | Fat: 24g | Saturated Fat: 5.6g | Carbohydrates: 22.7g | Sugar: 16.3g | Protein: 65.6g

⏰ Prep Time 15 m | ⏰ Cooking Time 12 m | 2 Servings

Ingredients:

- 2 (6-ounce) chicken breasts
- Salt and freshly ground black pepper, to taste
- ¾ cup oats
- 2 tablespoons mustard powder
- 1 tablespoon fresh parsley
- 2 medium eggs

Instructions:

1. Place the chicken breasts onto a cutting board and with a meat mallet, flatten each into even thickness.
2. Then, cut each breast in half.
3. Sprinkle the chicken pieces with salt and black pepper and set aside.
4. In a blender, add the oats, mustard powder, parsley, salt and black pepper and pulse until a coarse breadcrumb-like mixture is formed.
5. Transfer the oat mixture into a shallow bowl.
6. In another bowl, crack the eggs and beat well.
7. Coat the chicken breasts with oats mixture and then, dip into beaten eggs and again, coat with the oats mixture.
8. Arrange the "Crisper Basket" in the pot of Ninja Foodi Grill.
9. Close the Ninja Foodi Grill with lid and select "Air Crisp".
10. Set the temperature to 350 degrees F to preheat.
11. Press "Start/Stop" to begin preheating.
12. When the display shows "Add Food" open the lid and place the chicken breasts into the "Crisper Basket".
13. Close the Ninja Foodi Grill with lid and set the time for 12 minutes.
14. Press "Start/Stop" to begin cooking.
15. While cooking, flip the chicken breasts once halfway through.
16. When the cooking time is completed, press "Start/Stop" to stop cooking and open the lid.
17. Place the chicken breasts onto a serving platter for about 5 minutes before serving.

Nutritional Information per Serving:

Calories: 556 | Fat: 22.2g | Saturated Fat: 5.3g | Carbohydrates: 25.1g | Sugar: 1.40g | Protein: 61.6g

⏰ Prep Time 15 m | ⏰ Cooking Time 20 m | 4 Servings

Ingredients:

- 1 tablespoon sugar
- 8 fresh basil leaves
- 2 tablespoons red boat fish sauce
- 2 tablespoons water
- 2 (8-ounce) boneless chicken breasts, cut each breast in half horizontally
- Salt and freshly ground black pepper, to taste
- 8 bacon strips
- 1 tablespoon honey

Instructions:

1. In a small heavy-bottomed pan, add sugar over medium-low heat and cook for about 2-3 minutes or until caramelized, stirring continuously.
2. Stir in the basil, fish sauce and water.
3. Remove from heat and transfer into a large bowl.
4. Sprinkle the chicken with salt and black pepper.
5. Add the chicken pieces in basil mixture and coat generously.
6. Refrigerate to marinate for about 4-6 hours.
7. Wrap each chicken piece with 2 bacon strips.
8. Coat each chicken piece with honey slightly.
9. Arrange the greased "Crisper Basket" in the pot of Ninja Foodi Grill.
10. Close the Ninja Foodi Grill with lid and select "Air Crisp".
11. Set the temperature to 365 degrees F to preheat.
12. Press "Start/Stop" to begin preheating.
13. When the display shows "Add Food" open the lid and place the chicken breasts into the "Crisper Basket".
14. Close the Ninja Foodi Grill with lid and set the time for 20 minutes.
15. Press "Start/Stop" to begin cooking.
16. When the cooking time is completed, press "Start/Stop" to stop cooking and open the lid.
17. Serve hot.

Nutritional Information per Serving:

Calories: 564 | Fat: 32.6g | Saturated Fat: 10.3g | Carbohydrates: 8.2g | Sugar: 7.3g | Protein: 56.3g

⏰ Prep Time 10 m | ⏱ Cooking Time 15 m | 4 Servings

Ingredients:

- 4 (4-ounce) skinless, boneless chicken breasts
- 4 sausage links, casing removed

Instructions:

1. With a rolling pin, roll each chicken breast for about 1 minute.
2. Arrange the chicken breasts onto a smooth surface.
3. Place 1 sausage over each chicken breast.
4. Roll each breast around the sausage and secure with toothpicks.
5. Arrange the greased "Crisper Basket" in the pot of Ninja Foodi Grill.
6. Close the Ninja Foodi Grill with lid and select "Air Crisp".
7. Set the temperature to 375 degrees F to preheat.
8. Press "Start/Stop" to begin preheating.
9. When the display shows "Add Food" open the lid and place the chicken breasts into the "Crisper Basket".
10. Close the Ninja Foodi Grill with lid and set the time for 15 minutes.
11. Press "Start/Stop" to begin cooking.
12. When cooking time is completed, press "Start/Stop" to stop cooking and open the lid.
13. Serve hot.

Nutritional Information per Serving:

Calories: 430 | Fat: 28.2g | Saturated Fat: 9.3g | Carbohydrates: 0g | Sugar: 0g | Protein: 41.8g

⏰ Prep Time 15 m | ⏰ Cooking Time 30 m | 2 Servings

Ingredients:

- 1 tablespoon olive oil
- 1¾ ounces fresh spinach
- ¼ cup ricotta cheese, shredded
- 2 (4-ounce) skinless, boneless chicken breasts
- Salt and freshly ground black pepper, to taste
- 2 tablespoons cheddar cheese, grated
- ¼ teaspoon paprika

Instructions:

1. In a skillet, heat the oil over medium heat and cook the spinach for about 3-4 minutes.
2. Stir in the ricotta and cook for about 40-60 seconds.
3. Remove from heat and transfer the spinach mixture into a bowl. Set aside to cool.
4. Cut slits into the chicken breasts about ¼-inch apart but not all the way through.
5. Stuff each chicken breast with the spinach mixture.
6. Sprinkle each chicken breast with salt and black pepper and then with cheddar cheese and paprika.
7. Arrange the greased "Crisper Basket" in the pot of Ninja Foodi Grill.
8. Close the Ninja Foodi Grill with lid and select "Air Crisp".
9. Set the temperature to 390 degrees F to preheat.
10. Press "Start/Stop" to begin preheating.
11. When the display shows "Add Food" open the lid and place the chicken breasts into the "Crisper Basket".
12. Close the Ninja Foodi Grill with lid and set the time for 25 minutes.
13. Press "Start/Stop" to begin cooking.
14. When cooking time is completed, press "Start/Stop" to stop cooking and open the lid.
15. Serve hot.

Nutritional Information per Serving:

Calories: 279 | Fat: 16g | Saturated Fat: 5.6g | Carbohydrates: 2.7g | Sugar: 0.3g | Protein: 31.4g

⏰ Prep Time 15 m | ⏱ Cooking Time 30 m | 2 Servings

Ingredients:

- 2 (6-ounce) boneless, skinless chicken breast halves, pounded into ¼-inch thickness
- 2 (¾-ounce) deli ham slices
- 2 Swiss cheese slices
- ½ cup all-purpose flour
- 1/8 teaspoon paprika
- Salt and freshly ground black pepper, to taste
- 1 large egg
- 2 tablespoons 2% milk
- ½ cup seasoned breadcrumbs
- 1 tablespoon olive oil
- 1 tablespoon butter, melted

Instructions:

1. Arrange the chicken breast halves onto a smooth surface.
2. Arrange 1 ham slice over each chicken breast half, followed by the cheese.
3. Roll up each chicken breast half and tuck in ends.
4. With toothpicks, secure the rolls.
5. In a shallow plate, mix together the flour, paprika, salt and black pepper.
6. In a shallow bowl, place the egg and milk and beat slightly.
7. In a second shallow plate, place the breadcrumbs.
8. Coat each chicken roll with flour mixture, then dip into egg mixture and finally coat with breadcrumbs.
9. In a small skillet, heat the oil over medium heat and cook the chicken rolls for about 3-5 minutes or until browned from all sides.
10. Transfer the chicken rolls into the greased baking pan.
11. Arrange the "Crisper Basket" in the pot of Ninja Foodi Grill.
12. Close the Ninja Foodi Grill with lid and select "Bake".
13. Set the temperature to 350 degrees F to preheat.
14. Press "Start/Stop" to begin preheating.
15. When the display shows "Add Food" open the lid and place the pan into the "Crisper Basket".
16. Close the Ninja Foodi Grill with lid and set the time for 25 minutes.
17. Press "Start/Stop" to begin cooking.
18. When the cooking time is completed, press "Start/Stop" to stop cooking and open the lid.
19. Place the chicken rolls onto a platter and discard the toothpicks.
20. Drizzle with melted butter and serve.

Nutritional Information per Serving:

Calories: 672 | Fat: 28g | Saturated Fat: 9.3g | Carbohydrates: 45.9g | Sugar: 3.4g | Protein: 56.2g

⏰ Prep Time 15 m | ⏰ Cooking Time 30 m | 4 Servings

Ingredients:

- ¾ cup flour
- 2 large eggs
- 1½ cups breadcrumbs
- ¼ cup Parmesan cheese, grated
- 1 tablespoon mustard powder
- Salt and freshly ground black pepper, to taste
- 4 (6-ounces) (¼-inch thick) skinless, boneless chicken cutlets
- 1 lemon, cut into slices

Instructions:

1. In a shallow bowl, add the flour.
2. In a second bowl, crack the eggs and beat well.
3. In a third bowl, mix together the breadcrumbs, cheese, mustard powder, salt, and black pepper.
4. Season the chicken cutlets with salt, and black pepper.
5. Coat the chicken with flour, then dip into beaten eggs and finally coat with the breadcrumb mixture.
6. Arrange the greased "Crisper Basket" in the pot of Ninja Foodi
7. Close the Ninja Foodi Grill with lid and select "Air Crisp".
8. Set the temperature to 355 degrees F to preheat.
9. Press "Start/Stop" to begin preheating.
10. When the display shows "Add Food" open the lid and place the chicken cutlets into the "Crisper Basket".
11. Close the Ninja Foodi Grill with lid and set the time for 30 minutes.
12. Press "Start/Stop" to begin cooking.
13. When the cooking time is completed, press "Start/Stop" to stop cooking and open the lid.
14. Serve hot with the topping of lemon slices.

Nutritional Information per Serving:

Calories: 526 | Fat: 13g | Saturated Fat: 4.2g | Carbohydrates: 48.6g | Sugar: 3g | Protein: 51.7g

🕐 Prep Time 15 m | 🕐 Cooking Time 7 m | 3 Servings

Ingredients:

- 4 scallions, chopped
- 1 tablespoon fresh ginger, finely grated
- 4 garlic cloves, minced
- 2 tablespoons fresh lime juice

- 2 tablespoons low-sodium soy sauce
- 1 tablespoon olive oil
- 2 teaspoons sugar
- Pinch of ground black pepper
- 1 pound chicken tenders

Instructions:

1. In a large baking pan, mix together the scallion, ginger, garlic, pineapple juice, soy sauce, oil, sesame seeds, and black pepper.
2. Thread chicken tenders onto the pre-soaked wooden skewers.
3. Add the skewers into the baking pan and coat with marinade evenly.
4. Cover and refrigerate for about 2 hours or overnight.
5. Arrange the greased "Crisper Basket" in the pot of Ninja Foodi Grill.
6. Close the Ninja Foodi Grill with lid and select "Air Crisp".
7. Set the temperature to 390 degrees to preheat.
8. Press "Start/Stop" to begin preheating.
9. When the display shows "Add Food" open the lid and place the skewers into the "Crisper Basket".
10. Close the Ninja Foodi Grill with lid and set the time for 7 minutes.
11. Press "Start/Stop" to begin cooking.
12. When the cooking time is completed, press "Start/Stop" to stop cooking and open the lid.
13. Serve hot.

Nutritional Information per Serving:

Calories: 360 | Fat: 16g | Saturated Fat: 3.8g | Carbohydrates: 7.5g | Sugar: 3.9g | Protein: 45.2g

⏰ Prep Time 20 m | ⏰ Cooking Time 18 m | 6 Servings

Ingredients:

- 6 (4-ounces) boneless, skinless chicken thighs, trimmed and cut into cubes
- 1 tablespoon jerk seasoning
- 3 large zucchinis, sliced
- 12 ounces white mushrooms, stems removed
- Salt and freshly ground black pepper, to taste
- 2-3 tablespoons jerk sauce

Instructions:

1. In a bowl, mix together the chicken cubes and jerk seasoning.
2. Cover the bowl and refrigerate overnight.
3. Sprinkle the zucchini slices, and mushrooms with salt and black pepper.
4. Thread the chicken and vegetables onto greased metal skewers.
5. Arrange the greased "Crisper Basket" in the pot of Ninja Foodi Grill.
6. Close the Ninja Foodi Grill with lid and select "Air Crisp".
7. Set the temperature of Ninja Foodi to 370 degrees to preheat.
8. Press "Start/Stop" to begin preheating.
9. When the display shows "Add Food" open the lid and place the half of the skewers into the "Crisper Basket".
10. Close the Ninja Foodi Grill with lid and set the time for 9 minutes.
11. Press "Start/Stop" to begin cooking.
12. Flip and coat the kabobs with jerk sauce once halfway through.
13. When the cooking time is completed, press "Start/Stop" to stop cooking and open the lid.
14. Transfer the skewers onto a platter.
15. Repeat with the remaining skewers.
16. Serve hot.

Nutritional Information per Serving:

Calories: 256 | Fat: 9g | Saturated Fat: 2.4g | Carbohydrates: 7.4g | Sugar: 3.9g | Protein: 36.6g

⏰ Prep Time 15 m | ⏱ Cooking Time 30 m | 6 Servings

Ingredients:

- 6 (4-ounce) boneless, skinless chicken breasts
- 1 teaspoon mustard powder
- ½ teaspoon paprika
- 1 teaspoon Worcestershire sauce
- 1 cup flour
- 1 small egg
- ½ cup breadcrumbs
- ¼ teaspoon dried parsley
- ¼ teaspoon dried tarragon
- ¼ teaspoon dried oregano
- 1 teaspoon dried garlic
- 1 teaspoon chicken seasoning
- ½ teaspoon cayenne pepper
- Salt and freshly ground black pepper, to taste

Instructions:

1. In a food processor, add the chicken breasts and pulse until minced.
2. Add the mustard, paprika, Worcester sauce, salt, and black pepper and pulse until well combined.
3. Make 4 equal-sized patties from the mixture.
4. In a shallow bowl, place the flour.
5. In a second bowl, crack the egg and beat well.
6. In a third bowl, mix well breadcrumbs, dried herbs, and spices.
7. Coat each chicken patty with flour, then dip into egg and finally, coat with breadcrumbs mixture.
8. Arrange the greased "Crisper Basket" in the pot of Ninja Foodi Grill.
9. Close the Ninja Foodi Grill with lid and select "Air Crisp".
10. Set the temperature to 355 degrees F to preheat.
11. Press "Start/Stop" to begin preheating.
12. When the display shows "Add Food" open the lid and place the chicken patties into the "Crisper Basket".
13. Close the Ninja Foodi Grill with lid and set the time for 30 minutes.
14. Press "Start/Stop" to begin cooking.
15. Flip the patties once halfway through.
16. When the cooking time is completed, press "Start/Stop" to stop cooking and open the lid.
17. Serve hot.

Nutritional Information per Serving:

Calories: 341 | Fat: 9.9g | Saturated Fat: 2.7g | Carbohydrates: 23.2g | Sugar: 0.9g | Protein: 37.2g

⏱ Prep Time 10 m | ⏱ Cooking Time 1 h 20 m | 6 Servings

Ingredients:

- 1 (2¾-pound) bone-in, skin-on turkey breast half
- Salt and freshly ground black pepper, to taste

Instructions:

1. Rub the turkey breast with the salt and black pepper evenly.
2. Arrange the turkey breast into a greased baking pan.
3. Arrange the "Crisper Basket" in the pot of Ninja Foodi Grill.
4. Close the Ninja Foodi Grill with lid and select "Roast".
5. Set the temperature to 450 degrees F to preheat.
6. Press "Start/Stop" to begin preheating.
7. When the display shows "Add Food" open the lid and place the pan into the "Crisper Basket".
8. Close the Ninja Foodi Grill with lid and set the time for 80 minutes.
9. Press "Start/Stop" to begin cooking.
10. When the cooking time is completed, press "Start/Stop" to stop cooking and open the lid.
11. Place the turkey breast onto a cutting board.
12. With a piece of foil, cover the turkey breast for about 20 minutes before slicing.
13. With a sharp knife, cut the turkey breast into desired sized slices and serve.

Nutritional Information per Serving:

Calories: 221 | Fat: 0.8g | Saturated Fat: 0g | Carbohydrates: 0g | Sugar: 0g | Protein: 51.6g

⏰ Prep Time 15 m | ⏱ Cooking Time 3 m | 3 Servings

Ingredients:

- 1 teaspoon dried thyme, crushed
- 1 teaspoon dried rosemary, crushed
- ½ teaspoon dried sage, crushed
- ½ teaspoon dark brown sugar
- ½ teaspoon garlic powder
- ½ teaspoon paprika
- Salt and freshly ground black pepper, to taste
- 1 (2½-pound) bone-in, skin-on turkey breast
- 1 tablespoon olive oil

Instructions:

1. In a bowl, mix together the herbs, brown sugar, spices, salt and black pepper.
2. Coat the turkey breast with oil and then rub with the herb mixture evenly.
3. Arrange the "Crisper Basket" in the pot of Ninja Foodi Grill.
4. Close the Ninja Foodi Grill with lid and select "Air Crisp".
5. Set the temperature to 360 degrees F to preheat.
6. Press "Start/Stop" to begin preheating.
7. When the display shows "Add Food" open the lid and place the turkey breasts, skin-side down into the "Crisper Basket".
8. Close the Ninja Foodi Grill with lid and set the time for 35 minutes.
9. Press "Start/Stop" to begin cooking.
10. Flip the turkey breast once after 18 minutes of cooking.
11. When the cooking time is completed, press "Start/Stop" to stop cooking and open the lid.
12. Place the turkey breast onto a cutting board for about 10 minutes before slicing.
13. With a sharp knife, cut the turkey breast into desired sized slices and serve.

Nutritional Information per Serving:

Calories: 440 | Fat: 11.1g | Saturated Fat: 2g | Carbohydrates: 17.5g | Sugar: 13.9g | Protein: 64.7g

⏰ Prep Time 15 m | ⏱ Cooking Time 40 m | 6 Servings

Ingredients:

- ¼ cup butter, softened
- 2 tablespoons fresh rosemary, chopped
- 2 tablespoon fresh thyme, chopped
- 2 tablespoons fresh sage, chopped
- 2 tablespoons fresh parsley, chopped
- Salt and freshly ground black pepper, to taste
- 1 (4-pound) bone-in, skin-on turkey breast
- 2 tablespoons olive oil

Instructions:

1. In a bowl, add the butter, herbs, salt and black pepper and mix well.
2. Rub the herb mixture under skin evenly.
3. Coat the outside of turkey breast with oil.
4. Place the turkey breast into the greased baking pan.
5. Arrange the "Crisper Basket" in the pot of Ninja Foodi Grill.
6. Close the Ninja Foodi Grill with lid and select "Bake".
7. Set the temperature to 350 degrees F to preheat.
8. Press "Start/Stop" to begin preheating.
9. When the display shows "Add Food" open the lid and place the pan into the "Crisper Basket".
10. Close the Ninja Foodi Grill with lid and set the time for 40 minutes.
11. Press "Start/Stop" to begin cooking.
12. When the cooking time is completed, press "Start/Stop" to stop cooking and open the lid.
13. Place the turkey breast onto a platter for about 5-10 minutes before slicing
14. With a sharp knife, cut the turkey breast into desired sized slices and serve.

Nutritional Information per Serving:

Calories: 333 | Fat: 37g | Saturated Fat: 12.4g | Carbohydrates: 1.8g | Sugar: 0.1g | Protein: 65.1g

⏰ Prep Time 15 m | ⏰ Cooking Time 55 m | 10 Servings

Ingredients:

- 1 (5-pound) boneless turkey breast
- Salt and freshly ground black pepper, to taste
- 3 tablespoons honey
- 2 tablespoon Dijon mustard
- 1 tablespoon butter, softened

Instructions:

1. Season the turkey breast with salt and black pepper generously and spray with cooking spray.
2. Arrange the greased "Crisper Basket" in the pot of Ninja Foodi Grill.
3. Close the Ninja Foodi Grill with lid and select "Air Crisp".
4. Set the temperature to 350 degrees F to preheat.
5. Press "Start/Stop" to begin preheating.
6. When the display shows "Add Food" open the lid and place the turkey breast into the "Crisper Basket".
7. Close the Ninja Foodi Grill with lid and set the time for 55 minutes.
8. Press "Start/Stop" to begin cooking.
9. Meanwhile, for glaze: in a bowl, mix together the maple syrup, mustard and butter.
10. Flip the turkey breast twice, first after 25 minutes and then after 37 minutes.
11. After 50 minutes of cooking, coat the turkey breast with the glaze.
12. When the cooking time is completed, press "Start/Stop" to stop cooking and open the lid.
13. Place the turkey breast onto a cutting board for about 5 minutes before slicing.
14. Cut into desired sized slices and serve.

Nutritional Information per Serving:

Calories: 252 | Fat: 2.3g | Saturated Fat: 0.7g | Carbohydrates: 5.4g | Sugar: 5.2g | Protein: 56.4g

⏱ Prep Time 15 m | ⏱ Cooking Time 25 m | 8 Servings

Ingredients:

- ¾ cup brine from a can of olives
- ½ cup buttermilk
- 3½ pounds boneless, skinless turkey breast
- 2 fresh thyme sprigs
- 1 fresh rosemary sprig

Instructions:

1. In a bowl, add the olive brine and buttermilk and beat until well combined.
2. In a resalable plastic bag, place the turkey breast, buttermilk mixture and herb sprigs.
3. Seal the bag and refrigerate for about 8 hours.
4. Remove the turkey breast from bag and set aside until it reaches room temperature.
5. Arrange the greased "Crisper Basket" in the pot of Ninja Foodi Grill.
6. Close the Ninja Foodi Grill with lid and select "Air Crisp".
7. Set the temperature to 350 degrees F to preheat.
8. Press "Start/Stop" to begin preheating.
9. When the display shows "Add Food" open the lid and place the turkey breasts into the "Crisper Basket".
10. Close the Ninja Foodi Grill with lid and set the time for 20-25 minutes.
11. Press "Start/Stop" to begin cooking.
12. Flip the turkey breast once after 15 minutes.
13. When cooking time is completed, press "Start/Stop" to stop cooking and open the lid.
14. Place the turkey breast onto a platter.
15. Cover the turkey breast loosely with a piece of foil for about 10-15 minutes before slicing.
16. Cut the turkey breast into desired sized slices and serve.

Nutritional Information per Serving:

Calories: 238 | Fat: 1.2g | Saturated Fat: 0.2g | Carbohydrates: 1.5g | Sugar: 0.7g | Protein: 49.6g

🕐 Prep Time 10 m | 🕐 Cooking Time 20 m | 4 Servings

Ingredients:

- 1 teaspoon dried thyme, crushed
- 1 teaspoon garlic powder
- Salt and freshly ground black pepper, to taste
- 1 (24-ounce) package boneless turkey breast tenderloins
- 2 tablespoon olive oil

Instructions:

1. In a small bowl, mix together the thyme, garlic powder, salt and black pepper.
2. Rub the turkey tenderloins with thyme mixture evenly.
3. In a skillet, heat the oil over medium heat and cook the turkey tenderloins for about 10 minutes or until golden brown.
4. Remove from the heat and transfer the turkey tenderloins onto a plate.
5. Arrange the "Crisper Basket" in the pot of Ninja Foodi Grill.
6. Close the Ninja Foodi Grill with lid and select "Bake".
7. Set the temperature to 350 degrees F to preheat.
8. Press "Start/Stop" to begin preheating.
9. When the display shows "Add Food" open the lid and place the turkey tenderloins into the "Crisper Basket".
10. Close the Ninja Foodi Grill with lid and set the time for 10 minutes.
11. Press "Start/Stop" to begin cooking.
12. When cooking time is completed, press "Start/Stop" to stop cooking and open the lid.
13. Place the turkey tenderloins onto a cutting board for about 5 minutes before slicing.
14. Cut into desired sized slices and serve.

Nutritional Information per Serving:

Calories: 244 | Fat: 9.2g | Saturated Fat: 1.7g | Carbohydrates: 0.7g | Sugar: 0.2g | Protein: 39.3g

⏰ Prep Time 15 m | ⏰ Cooking Time 40 m | 3 Servings

Ingredients:

- 1 pound turkey breast fillet
- 1 garlic clove, crushed
- 1½ teaspoons ground cumin
- 1 teaspoon ground cinnamon
- ½ teaspoon red chili powder
- Salt, to taste
- 2 tablespoons olive oil
- 3 tablespoons fresh parsley, chopped finely
- 1 small red onion, chopped finely

Instructions:

1. Place the turkey fillet on a cutting board.
2. Carefully cut horizontally along the length about 1/3 of way from the top, stopping about ¼-inch from the edge.
3. Open this part to have a long piece of fillet.
4. In a bowl, mix together the garlic, spices and oil.
5. In a small cup, reserve about 1 tablespoon of oil mixture.
6. In the remaining oil mixture, add the parsley and onion and mix well.
7. Coat the open side of fillet with onion mixture.
8. Roll the fillet tightly from the short side.
9. With a kitchen string, tie the roll at 1-1½-inch intervals.
10. Coat the outer side of roll with the reserved oil mixture.
11. Arrange the "Crisper Basket" in the pot of Ninja Foodi Grill.
12. Close the Ninja Foodi Grill with lid and select "Air Crisp".
13. Set the temperature to 355 degrees F to preheat.
14. Press "Start/Stop" to begin preheating.
15. When the display shows "Add Food" open the lid and place the turkey roll into the "Crisper Basket".
16. Close the Ninja Foodi Grill with lid and set the time for 40 minutes.
17. Press "Start/Stop" to begin cooking.
18. When cooking time is completed, press "Start/Stop" to stop cooking and open the lid.
19. Transfer the turkey roll onto a cutting board for about 5-10 minutes before slicing.
20. With a sharp knife, cut the turkey roll into desired sized slices and serve.

Nutritional Information per Serving:

Calories: 319 | Fat: 11.8g | Saturated Fat: 2.1g | Carbohydrates: 4.2g | Sugar: 1.3g | Protein: 50g

⏰ Prep Time 10 m | ⏱ Cooking Time 30 m | 2 Servings

Ingredients:

- 2 garlic cloves, minced
- 1 tablespoon fresh rosemary, minced
- 1 teaspoon fresh lime zest, finely grated
- 2 tablespoons olive oil
- 1 tablespoon fresh lime juice
- Salt and freshly ground black pepper, to taste
- 2 turkey legs

Instructions:

1. In a large bowl, mix together the garlic, rosemary, lime zest, oil, lime juice, salt, and black pepper.
2. Add the turkey legs and generously coat with marinade.
3. Refrigerate to marinate for about 6-8 hours.
4. Arrange the greased "Crisper Basket" in the pot of Ninja Foodi Grill.
5. Close the Ninja Foodi Grill with lid and select "Air Crisp".
6. Set the temperature to 350 degrees F to preheat.
7. Press "Start/Stop" to begin preheating.
8. When the display shows "Add Food" open the lid and place the turkey legs into the "Crisper Basket".
9. Close the Ninja Foodi Grill with lid and set the time for 30 minutes.
10. Press "Start/Stop" to begin cooking.
11. Flip the turkey legs once halfway through.
12. When the cooking time is completed, press "Start/Stop" to stop cooking and open the lid.
13. Serve hot.

Nutritional Information per Serving:

Calories: 709 | Fat: 32.7g | Saturated Fat: 7.8g | Carbohydrates: 2.3g | Sugar: 0.1g | Protein: 97.2g

⏰ Prep Time 10 m | ⏰ Cooking Time 26 m | 4 Servings

Ingredients:

- 2 pounds turkey wings
- 4 tablespoons chicken rub
- 3 tablespoons olive oil

Instructions:

1. In a large bowl, add the turkey wings, chicken rub and olive oil and toss to coat well.
2. Arrange the greased "Crisper Basket" in the pot of Ninja Foodi Grill.
3. Close the Ninja Foodi Grill with lid and select "Air Crisp".
4. Set the temperature to 380 degrees F to preheat.
5. Press "Start/Stop" to begin preheating.
6. When the display shows "Add Food" open the lid and place the turkey wings into the "Crisper Basket".
7. Close the Ninja Foodi Grill with lid and set the time for 26 minutes.
8. Press "Start/Stop" to begin cooking.
9. Flip the turkey wings once halfway through.
10. When the cooking time is completed, press "Start/Stop" to stop cooking and open the lid.
11. Serve hot.

Nutritional Information per Serving:

Calories: 558 | Fat: 38.9g | Saturated Fat: 1.5g | Carbohydrates: 3g | Sugar: 0g | Protein: 46.6g

⏰ Prep Time 15 m | ⏰ Cooking Time 15 m | 2 Servings

Ingredients:

- 8 ounces ground turkey breast
- 1½ tablespoons extra-virgin olive oil
- 2 garlic cloves, grated
- 2 teaspoons fresh oregano, chopped
- ½ teaspoon red pepper flakes, crushed
- Salt, to taste
- ¼ cup feta cheese, crumbled

Instructions:

1. In a large bowl, add all the ingredients except for cheese and mix until well combined.
2. Make 2 (½-inch-thick) patties from the mixture.
3. Arrange the greased "Crisper Basket" in the pot of Ninja Foodi Grill.
4. Close the Ninja Foodi Grill with lid and select "Air Crisp".
5. Set the temperature to 360 degrees F to preheat.
6. Press "Start/Stop" to begin preheating.
7. When the display shows "Add Food" open the lid and place the pan into the "Crisper Basket".
8. Close the Ninja Foodi Grill with lid and set the time for 15 minutes.
9. Press "Start/Stop" to begin cooking.
10. Flip the patties once halfway through.
11. When the cooking time is completed, press "Start/Stop" to stop cooking and open the lid.
12. Serve hot with the topping of feta.

Nutritional Information per Serving:

Calories: 364 | Fat: 23.1g | Saturated Fat: 6.7g | Carbohydrates: 3g | Sugar: 0.9g | Protein: 35.6g

⏰ Prep Time 10 m | ⏰ Cooking Time 25 m | 4 Servings

Ingredients:

- 6 eggs
- ½ cup plain Greek yogurt
- ½ cup cooked turkey meat, chopped
- Salt and freshly ground black pepper, to taste
- ½ cup sharp Cheddar cheese, shredded

Instructions:

1. In a bowl, add the egg and yogurt and beat well.
2. Add the remaining ingredients and stir to combine.
3. In a greased baking pan, place the egg mixture.
4. Arrange the "Crisper Basket" in the pot of Ninja Foodi Grill.
5. Close the Ninja Foodi Grill with lid and select "Bake".
6. Set the temperature to 375 degrees F to preheat.
7. Press "Start/Stop" to begin preheating.
8. When the display shows "Add Food" open the lid and place the pan into the "Crisper Basket".
9. Close the Ninja Foodi Grill with lid and set the time for 25 minutes.
10. Press "Start/Stop" to begin cooking.
11. When cooking time is completed, press "Start/Stop" to stop cooking and open the lid.
12. Serve warm.

Nutritional Information per Serving:

Calories: 203 | Fat: 12.4g | Saturated Fat: 5.6g | Carbohydrates: 2.9g | Sugar: 2.7g | Protein: 18.7g

⏰ Prep Time 15 m | ⏰ Cooking Time 1 h 5 m | 8 Servings

Ingredients:
For Meatloaf:

- 2 pounds lean ground turkey
- 1 cup quick-cooking oats
- ½ cup carrot, peeled and shredded
- 1 medium onion, chopped
- ½ cup fat-free milk
- ¼ of egg, beaten

- 2 tablespoons ketchup
- 1 teaspoon garlic powder
- ¼ teaspoon ground black pepper

For Topping:

- ¼ cup ketchup
- ¼ cup quick-cooking oats

Instructions:

1. For meatloaf: in a bowl, add all the ingredients and mix until well combined.
2. For topping: in another bowl, add all the ingredients and mix until well combined.
3. Transfer the mixture into a greased loaf pan and top with the topping mixture.
4. Arrange the "Crisper Basket" in the pot of Ninja Foodi Grill.
5. Close the Ninja Foodi Grill with lid and select "Bake".
6. Set the temperature to 350 degrees F to preheat.
7. Press "Start/Stop" to begin preheating.
8. When the display shows "Add Food" open the lid and place the pan into the "Crisper Basket".
9. Close the Ninja Foodi Grill with lid and set the time for 65 minutes.
10. Press "Start/Stop" to begin cooking.
11. When the cooking time is completed, press "Start/Stop" to stop cooking and open the lid.
12. Place the loaf pan onto a wire rack for about 10 minutes before slicing.
13. Carefully invert the loaf onto the wire rack.
14. Cut into desired sized slices and serve.

Nutritional Information per Serving:

Calories: 239 | Fat: 9.1g | Saturated Fat: 2.7g | Carbohydrates: 14.5g | Sugar: 4.5g | Protein: 25.1g

⏰ Prep Time 15 m | ⏰ Cooking Time 20 m | 2 Servings

Ingredients:

- 1 (10½-ounce) duck breast
- 1 tablespoon wholegrain mustard
- 1 teaspoon honey
- 1 teaspoon balsamic vinegar
- Salt and freshly ground black pepper, to taste

Instructions:

1. Arrange the "Crisper Basket" in the pot of Ninja Foodi Grill.
2. Close the Ninja Foodi Grill with lid and select "Air Crisp".
3. Set the temperature to 365 degrees F to preheat.
4. Press "Start/Stop" to begin preheating.
5. When the display shows "Add Food" open the lid and place the duck breast, skin side up into the "Crisper Basket".
6. Close the Ninja Foodi Grill with lid and set the time for 20 minutes.
7. Press "Start/Stop" to begin cooking.
8. Meanwhile, in a bowl, mix together the remaining ingredients.
9. After 15 minutes of cooking, coat the duck breast with the honey mixture generously.
10. When the cooking time is completed, press "Start/Stop" to stop cooking and open the lid.
11. Place the duck breast onto a cutting board.
12. Cut into 2 portions and serve hot.

Nutritional Information per Serving:

Calories: 229 | Fat: 7.6g | Saturated Fat: 0.1g | Carbohydrates: 4.9g | Sugar: 3.3g | Protein: 34.2g

⏰ Prep Time 15 m | ⏰ Cooking Time 20 m | 2 Servings

Ingredients:

- 1 (10-ounce) duck breast
- Olive oil cooking spray
- ½ tablespoon fresh thyme, chopped
- ½ tablespoon fresh rosemary, chopped
- 1 cup chicken broth
- 1 tablespoon fresh lemon juice
- Salt and freshly ground black pepper, to taste

Instructions:

1. Spray the duck breast with cooking spray evenly.
2. In a bowl, mix well the remaining ingredients.
3. Add the duck breast and coat with the marinade generously.
4. Refrigerate, covered for about 4 hours.
5. Arrange the greased "Crisper Basket" in the pot of Ninja Foodi Grill.
6. Close the Ninja Foodi Grill with lid and select "Air Crisp".
7. Set the temperature to 390 degrees F to preheat.
8. Press "Start/Stop" to begin preheating.
9. When the display shows "Add Food" open the lid and place the duck breast into the "Crisper Basket".
10. Close the Ninja Foodi Grill with lid and set the time for 15 minutes.
11. Press "Start/Stop" to begin cooking.
12. After 15 minutes of cooking, remove the foil from the breast.
13. Now, set the temperature to 355 degrees F for 5 minutes.
14. When the cooking time is completed, press "Start/Stop" to stop cooking and open the lid.
15. Serve hot.

Nutritional Information per Serving:

Calories: 209 | Fat: 6.6g | Saturated Fat: 0.3g | Carbohydrates: 1.6g | Sugar: 0.5g | Protein: 33.8g

⏰ Prep Time 10 m | ⏰ Cooking Time 30 m | 2 Servings

Ingredients:

- 2 garlic cloves, minced
- 1 tablespoon fresh parsley, chopped
- 1 teaspoon five spice powder
- Salt and freshly ground black pepper, to taste
- 2 duck legs

Instructions:

1. In a bowl, mix together the garlic, parsley, five spice powder, salt and black pepper.
2. Rub the duck legs with garlic mixture generously.
3. Arrange the "Crisper Basket" in the pot of Ninja Foodi Grill.
4. Close the Ninja Foodi Grill with lid and select "Air Crisp".
5. Set the temperature to 340 degrees F to preheat.
6. Press "Start/Stop" to begin preheating.
7. When the display shows "Add Food" open the lid and place the duck legs into the "Crisper Basket".
8. Close the Ninja Foodi Grill with lid and set the time for 25 minutes.
9. Press "Start/Stop" to begin cooking.
10. After 25 minutes, set the temperature to 390 degrees F for 5 minutes.
11. When the cooking time is completed, press "Start/Stop" to stop cooking and open the lid.
12. Serve hot.

Nutritional Information per Serving:

Calories: 434 | Fat: 14.4g | Saturated Fat: 3.2g | Carbohydrates: 1.1g | Sugar: 0.1g | Protein: 70.4g

⏰ Prep Time 10 m | ⏱ Cooking Time 40 m | 8 Servings

Ingredients:

- 1 (3-pound) beef tenderloin, trimmed
- 2 tablespoons olive oil
- Salt and freshly ground black pepper, to taste

Instructions:

1. Arrange a wire rack in a baking pan.
2. Rub tenderloin with oil and then season with salt and black pepper evenly.
3. Place the tenderloin into the prepared baking pan.
4. Arrange the "Crisper Basket" in the pot of Ninja Foodi Grill.
5. Close the Ninja Foodi Grill with lid and select "Bake".
6. Set the temperature to 400 degrees F to preheat.
7. Press "Start/Stop" to begin preheating.
8. When the display shows "Add Food" open the lid and place the <u>pan</u> into the "Crisper Basket".
9. Close the Ninja Foodi Grill with lid and set the time for 40 minutes.
10. Press "Start/Stop" to begin cooking.
11. When the cooking time is completed, press "Start/Stop" to stop cooking and open the lid.
12. Place the tenderloin onto a cutting board.
13. With a piece of foil, cover the tenderloin for about 10 minutes before slicing.
14. With a sharp knife, cut the tenderloin into desired sized slices and serve.

Nutritional Information per Serving:

Calories: 380 | Fat: 19.1g | Saturated Fat: 6.4g | Carbohydrates: 0g | Sugar: 0g | Protein: 49.2g

⏰ Prep Time 15 m | ⏰ Cooking Time 12 m | 4 Servings

Ingredients:

- 8 bacon strips
- 4 (8-ounce) center-cut beef tenderloin filets
- 2 tablespoons 0live oil, divided
- Salt and freshly ground black pepper, to taste

Instructions:

1. Wrap 2 bacon strips around the entire outside of each beef filet.
2. With toothpicks, secure each filet.
3. Coat each wrapped filet with oil and sprinkle with salt and black pepper evenly.
4. Arrange the "Grill Grate" in the pot of Ninja Foodi Grill.
5. Close the Ninja Foodi Grill with lid and select "Grill" to preheat.
6. Press "Start/Stop" to begin preheating.
7. When the display shows "Add Food" open the lid and place the wrapped tenderloin onto the "Grill Grate".
8. Close the Ninja Foodi Grill with lid and set the time for 12 minutes.
9. Press "Start/Stop" to begin cooking.
10. After 6 minutes of cooking, flip the tenderloin.
11. When the cooking time is completed, press "Start/Stop" to stop cooking and open the lid.
12. Transfer the tenderloin onto a platter for about 10 minutes before serving.
13. With a sharp knife, cut the tenderloin into desired sized slices and serve.

Nutritional Information per Serving:

Calories: 841 | Fat: 52g | Saturated Fat: 16.9g | Carbohydrates: 0.8g | Sugar: 1g | Protein: 87.1g

⏰ Prep Time 15 m | ⏰ Cooking Time 3 h | 3 Servings

Ingredients:

- ¾ pound beef round, trimmed
- ¼ cup Worcestershire sauce
- ¼ cup low-sodium soy sauce
- 1 teaspoon honey
- ½ teaspoon liquid smoke
- 1 teaspoon onion powder
- ¼ teaspoon red pepper flakes
- Ground black pepper, to taste

Instructions:

1. In a zip-top bag, place the beef and freeze for 1-2 hours to firm up.
2. Place the meat onto a cutting board and cut against the grain into 1/8-¼-inch strips.
3. In a large bowl, add the remaining ingredients and mix until well combined.
4. Add the steak slices and coat with the mixture generously.
5. Refrigerate to marinate for about 4-6 hours.
6. Remove the beef slices from bowl and with paper towels, pat dry them.
7. Place the steak strips onto a baking pan and arrange in an even layer.
8. Arrange the "Crisper Basket" in the pot of Ninja Foodi Grill.
9. Close the Ninja Foodi Grill with lid and select "Dehydrate"
10. Set the temperature to 160 degrees F to preheat.
11. Press "Start/Stop" to begin preheating.
12. When the display shows "Add Food" open the lid and place the pan into the "Crisper Basket".
13. Close the Ninja Foodi Grill with lid and set the time for 1½ hours.
14. Press "Start/Stop" to begin cooking.
15. When the cooking time is completed, press "Start/Stop" to stop cooking and open the lid.
16. Set the baking pan aside to cool completely before serving.

Nutritional Information per Serving:

Calories: 372 | Fat: 10.7g | Saturated Fat: 4g | Carbohydrates: 12g | Sugar: 11.3g | Protein: 53.8g

⏰ Prep Time 10 m | ⏱ Cooking Time 18 m | 2 Servings

Ingredients:

- 2 (6-ounce) (½-inch thick) pork chops
- Salt and freshly ground black pepper, to taste

Instructions:

1. Season the both sides of the pork chops with salt and black pepper generously.
2. Arrange the pork chops into a greased baking pan.
3. Arrange the "Grill Grate" in the pot of Ninja Foodi Grill.
4. Close the Ninja Foodi Grill with lid and select "Grill" on "Medium" to preheat.
5. Press "Start/Stop" to begin preheating.
6. When the display shows "Add Food" open the lid and place the baking pan onto the "Grill Grate".
7. With your hands, gently press down each pork chop.
8. Close the Ninja Foodi Grill with lid and set the time for 18 minutes.
9. Press "Start/Stop" to begin cooking.
10. After 12 minutes of cooking, flip the chops once.
11. When the cooking time is completed, press "Start/Stop" to stop cooking and open the lid.
12. Serve hot.

Nutritional Information per Serving:

Calories: 544 | Fat: 42.3g | Saturated Fat: 15.8g | Carbohydrates: 0g | Sugar: 0g | Protein: 38.2g

⏰ Prep Time 10 m | ⏰ Cooking Time 12 m | 4 Servings

Ingredients:

- 4 (6-ounce) boneless pork chops
- 2 tablespoons pork rub
- 1 tablespoon olive oil

Instructions:

1. Coat both sides of the pork chops with the oil and then, rub with the pork rub.
2. Place the pork chops onto the lightly greased baking pan.
3. Arrange the "Crisper Basket" in the pot of Ninja Foodi Grill.
4. Close the Ninja Foodi Grill with lid and select "Air Crisp".
5. Set the temperature to 400 degrees F to preheat.
6. Press "Start/Stop" to begin preheating.
7. When the display shows "Add Food" open the lid and place the pan into the "Crisper Basket".
8. Close the Ninja Foodi Grill with lid and set the time for 12 minutes.
9. Press "Start/Stop" to begin cooking.
10. Flip the chops once halfway through.
11. When the cooking time is completed, press "Start/Stop" to stop cooking and open the lid.
12. Serve hot.

Nutritional Information per Serving:

Calories: 285 | Fat: 9.5g | Saturated Fat: 2.5g | Carbohydrates: 1.5g | Sugar: 0.8g | Protein: 44.5g

⏰ Prep Time 10 m | ⏱ Cooking Time 15 m | 2 Servings

Ingredients:

- 2 bacon slices
- 2 (6-ounces) filet mignon

- Salt and freshly ground black pepper, to taste
- 1 teaspoon avocado oil

Instructions:

1. Wrap 1 bacon slice around each mignon steak and secure with a toothpick.
2. Season the steak evenly with salt and black pepper.
3. Then, coat each filet with avocado oil.
4. Arrange the greased "Crisper Basket" in the pot of Ninja Foodi Grill.
5. Close the Ninja Foodi Grill with lid and select "Air Crisp".
6. Set the temperature to 375 degrees F to preheat.
7. Press "Start/Stop" to begin preheating.
8. When the display shows "Add Food" open the lid and place the filets into the "Crisper Basket".
9. Close the Ninja Foodi Grill with lid and set the time for 15 minutes.
10. Press "Start/Stop" to begin cooking.
11. Flip the filets once halfway through.
12. When the cooking time is completed, press "Start/Stop" to stop cooking and open the lid.
13. Serve hot.

Nutritional Information per Serving:

Calories: 464 | Fat: 23.6g | Saturated Fat: 8.3g | Carbohydrates: 0.5g | Sugar: 0g | Protein: 58.5g

Prep Time 15 m | Cooking Time 10 m | 4 Servings

Ingredients:

- 1¼ pounds skirt steak
- ½ cup low-sodium soy sauce
- ¼ cup white wine
- 3-4 tablespoons fresh lemon juice

- 2 tablespoons sesame oil
- 3 tablespoons maple syrup
- 1 tablespoon red pepper flakes, crushed
- 2 garlic cloves, minced

Instructions:

1. In a large resealable bag, place all the ingredients except for the scallions.
2. Seal the bag and shake to mix well.
3. Refrigerate for up to 2 hours.
4. Remove the steak from bag and set aside at room temperature for 20 minutes before cooking.
5. Place the skirt steak into a greased baking pan.
6. Arrange the "Crisper Basket" in the pot of Ninja Foodi Grill.
7. Close the Ninja Foodi Grill with lid and select "Bake"
8. Set the temperature to 400 degrees F to preheat.
9. Press "Start/Stop" to begin preheating.
10. When the display shows "Add Food" open the lid and place the pan into the "Crisper Basket".
11. Close the Ninja Foodi Grill with lid and set the time for 10 minutes.
12. Press "Start/Stop" to begin cooking.
13. When the cooking time is completed, press "Start/Stop" to stop cooking and open the lid.
14. Place the steak onto a cutting board for about 10-15 minutes before slicing.
15. With a sharp knife, cut the steak into desired sized slices and serve.

Nutritional Information per Serving:

Calories: 421 | Fat: 21.4g | Saturated Fat: 6.6g | Carbohydrates: 14g | Sugar: 11.5g | Protein: 40.2g

🕐 Prep Time 15 m | 🕐 Cooking Time 14 m | 3 Servings

Ingredients:

- ½ cup unsalted butter, softened
- 2 tablespoons fresh parsley, chopped
- 2 teaspoons garlic, minced
- 1 teaspoon Worcestershire sauce
- Salt, to taste
- 2 (8-ounce) rib eye steaks
- Ground black pepper, to taste
- 1 tablespoon olive oil

Instructions:

1. Place the butter, parsley, garlic, Worcestershire sauce and salt in a bowl and mix until well combined.
2. Place the butter mixture onto a parchment paper and roll into a log.
3. Refrigerate until using.
4. Coat the steak with oil and then, sprinkle with salt and black pepper evenly.
5. Arrange the "Crisper Basket" in the pot of Ninja Foodi Grill.
6. Close the Ninja Foodi Grill with lid and select "Bake".
7. Set the temperature to 400 degrees F to preheat.
8. Press "Start/Stop" to begin preheating.
9. When the display shows "Add Food" open the lid and place the steaks into the "Crisper Basket".
10. Close the Ninja Foodi Grill with lid and set the time for 14 minutes.
11. Press "Start/Stop" to begin cooking.
12. Flip the steaks once halfway through.
13. When the cooking time is completed, press "Start/Stop" to stop cooking and open the lid.
14. Place the steaks onto a platter for about 5 minutes.
15. Cut each steak into desired sized slices and divide onto serving plates.
16. Now, cut the butter log into slices.
17. Top each steak with butter slices and serve.

Nutritional Information per Serving:

Calories: 637 | Fat: 51.4g | Saturated Fat: 25.4g | Carbohydrates: 1.2g | Sugar: 0.4g | Protein: 41.4g

⏰ Prep Time 10 m | ⏰ Cooking Time 12 m | 8 Servings

Ingredients:

- 2 (1½-pound) rib-eye steaks
- 3-4 tablespoons steak seasoning
- Salt and freshly ground black pepper, to taste

Instructions:

1. Season steaks with steak seasoning, salt and black pepper.
2. Set aside at room temperature for about 30 minutes.
3. Arrange the greased "Grill Grate" in the pot of Ninja Foodi Grill.
4. Close the Ninja Foodi Grill with lid and select "Grill" to "High" to preheat.
5. Press "Start/Stop" to begin preheating.
6. When the display shows "Add Food" open the lid and place the steaks onto the "Grill Grate".
7. With your hands, gently press down each steak.
8. Close the Ninja Foodi Grill with lid and set the time for 12 minutes.
9. Press "Start/Stop" to begin cooking.
10. After 6 minutes of cooking, flip the steaks.
11. When cooking time is completed, press "Start/Stop" to stop cooking and open the lid.
12. Place the steaks onto a cutting board for about 5 minutes before slicing.
13. Cut into desired sized slices and serve.

Nutritional Information per Serving:

Calories: 467 | Fat: 37.6g | Saturated Fat: 15.1g | Carbohydrates: 0g | Sugar: 0g | Protein: 30.1g

⏰ Prep Time 10 m | ⏰ Cooking Time 8 m | 4 Servings

Ingredients:

- 2 (14-ounce) New York strip steaks
- 2 tablespoons butter, melted
- Salt and freshly ground black pepper, to taste

Instructions:

1. Brush each steak with the melted butter and season with salt and black pepper.
2. Arrange the greased "Grill Grate" in the pot of Ninja Foodi Grill.
3. Close the Ninja Foodi Grill with lid and select "Grill" to "High" to preheat.
4. Press "Start/Stop" to begin preheating.
5. When the display shows "Add Food" open the lid and place the steaks onto the "Grill Grate".
6. With your hands, gently press down each steak.
7. Close the Ninja Foodi Grill with lid and set the time for 8 minutes.
8. Press "Start/Stop" to begin cooking.
9. After 4 minutes of cooking, flip the steaks.
10. When the cooking time is completed, press "Start/Stop" to stop cooking and open the lid.
11. Place the steaks onto a cutting board for about 5 minutes before slicing.
12. Cut each steak into desired sized slices and serve.

Nutritional Information per Serving:

Calories: 296 | Fat: 12.7g | Saturated Fat: 6.6g | Carbohydrates: 0g | Sugar: 0g | Protein: 44.5g

Prep Time 10 m | Cooking Time 8 m | 2 Servings

Ingredients:

- ¼ teaspoon smoked paprika
- 1/8 teaspoon cayenne pepper
- 1/8 teaspoon ground cumin
- Salt and freshly ground black pepper, to taste
- 1 (9½-ounces) New York strip steak
- 1 teaspoon olive oil

Instructions:

1. In a small bowl, mix together the spice, salt and black pepper.
2. Coat the steak with oil and then, rub with spice mixture evenly.
3. Arrange the "Crisper Basket" in the pot of Ninja Foodi Grill.
4. Close the Ninja Foodi Grill with lid and select "Air Crisp".
5. Set the temperature to 400 degrees F to preheat.
6. Press "Start/Stop" to begin preheating.
7. When the display shows "Add Food" open the lid and place the steak into the "Crisper Basket".
8. Close the Ninja Foodi Grill with lid and set the time for 8 minutes.
9. Press "Start/Stop" to begin cooking.
10. When the cooking time is completed, press "Start/Stop" to stop cooking and open the lid.
11. place the steak onto a cutting board for about 10 minutes before slicing.
12. Cut the steak into desired sized slices and serve.
1. Serve immediately.

Instructions:

1. In a large resealable bag, place all the ingredients except for the scallions.
2. Seal the bag and shake to mix well.
3. Refrigerate for up to 2 hours.
4. Remove the steak from bag and set aside at room temperature for 20 minutes before cooking.

Nutritional Information per Serving:

Calories: 288 | Fat: 14.5g | Saturated Fat: 4.8g | Carbohydrates: 0.3g | Sugar: 0g | Protein: 36.9g

⏲ Prep Time 15 m | ⏲ Cooking Time 12 m | 6 Servings

Ingredients:

- 2 pounds flank steak
- 3 tablespoons fresh lemon juice
- 2 tablespoons olive oil
- 3 garlic cloves, minced
- 1 teaspoon red chili powder
- Salt and freshly ground black pepper, to taste

Instructions:

1. In a large bowl, add all the ingredients except for steak and mix well.
2. Add the flank steak and coat with the marinade generously.
3. Refrigerate to marinate for 24 hours, flipping occasionally.
4. Arrange the steak into a greased baking pan.
5. Arrange the greased "Grill Grate" in the pot of Ninja Foodi Grill.
6. Close the Ninja Foodi Grill with lid and select "Grill" to "High" to preheat.
7. Press "Start/Stop" to begin preheating.
8. When the display shows "Add Food" open the lid and place the steak onto the "Grill Grate".
9. With your hands, gently press down the steak.
10. Close the Ninja Foodi Grill with lid and set the time for 12 minutes.
11. Press "Start/Stop" to begin cooking.
12. Flip the steak once halfway through.
13. When the cooking time is completed, press "Start/Stop" to stop cooking and open the lid.
14. Place the steak onto a cutting board for about 10-15 minutes before slicing.
15. With a sharp knife, cut the roast into desired sized slices and serve.

Nutritional Information per Serving:

Calories: 339 | Fat: 17.4g | Saturated Fat: 6g | Carbohydrates: 0.9g | Sugar: 0.2g | Protein: 42.3g

⏰ Prep Time 10 m | ⏰ Cooking Time 16 m | 6 Servings

Ingredients:

- 6 (8-ounce) pork loin chops
- Salt and freshly ground black pepper, to taste
- ½ cup BBQ sauce

Instructions:

1. With a meat mallet, pound the chops completely.
2. Sprinkle the chops with a little salt and black pepper.
3. In a large bowl, add the BBQ sauce and chops and mix well.
4. Refrigerate, covered for about 6-8 hours.
5. Arrange the "Crisper Basket" in the pot of Ninja Foodi Grill.
6. Close the Ninja Foodi Grill with lid and select "Air Crisp".
7. Set the temperature to 355 degrees F to preheat.
8. Press "Start/Stop" to begin preheating.
9. When the display shows "Add Food" open the lid and place the chops into the "Crisper Basket".
10. Close the Ninja Foodi Grill with lid and set the time for 16 minutes.
11. Press "Start/Stop" to begin cooking.
12. After 8 minutes of cooking, flip the chops.
13. When the cooking time is completed, press "Start/Stop" to stop cooking and open the lid.
14. Serve hot.

Nutritional Information per Serving:

Calories: 757 | Fat: 56.4g | Saturated Fat: 21.1g | Carbohydrates: 7.6g | Sugar: 5.4g | Protein: 51g

⏰ Prep Time 15 m | ⏰ Cooking Time 12 m | 4 Servings

Ingredients:

- 2 garlic cloves, minced
- ½ tablespoon fresh cilantro, chopped
- ½ tablespoon fresh rosemary, chopped
- ½ tablespoon fresh parsley, chopped
- 2 tablespoons olive oil

- ¾ tablespoon Dijon mustard
- 1 tablespoon ground coriander
- 1 teaspoon sugar
- Salt, to taste
- 2 (6-ounces) (1-inch thick) pork chops

Instructions:

1. In a bowl, mix together the garlic, herbs, oil, mustard, coriander, sugar, and salt.
2. Add the pork chops and coat with marinade generously.
3. Cover and refrigerate for about 2-3 hours.
4. Remove chops from the refrigerator and set aside at room temperature for about 30 minutes.
5. Arrange the "Crisper Basket" in the pot of Ninja Foodi Grill.
6. Close the Ninja Foodi Grill with lid and select "Air Crisp".
7. Set the temperature to 390 degrees F to preheat.
8. Press "Start/Stop" to begin preheating.
9. When the display shows "Add Food" open the lid and place the chops into the "Crisper Basket".
10. Close the Ninja Foodi Grill with lid and set the time for 12 minutes.
11. Press "Start/Stop" to begin cooking.
12. When the cooking time is completed, press "Start/Stop" to stop cooking and open the lid.
13. Serve hot.

Nutritional Information per Serving:

Calories: 467 | Fat: 25.7g | Saturated Fat: 5.9g | Carbohydrates: 3.9g | Sugar: 2.1g | Protein: 53.5g

⏰ Prep Time 15 m | ⏰ Cooking Time 15 m | 3 Servings

Ingredients:

- 3 (6-ounce) pork chops
- Salt and freshly ground black pepper, to taste
- ¼ cup plain flour
- 1 egg
- 4 ounces seasoned breadcrumbs
- 1 tablespoon canola oil

Instructions:

1. Season each pork chop with salt and black pepper.
2. In a shallow bowl, place the flour
3. In a second bowl, crack the egg and beat well.
4. In a third bowl, add the breadcrumbs and oil and mix until a crumbly mixture forms.
5. Coat the pork chops with flour, then dip into beaten egg and finally, coat with the breadcrumbs mixture.
6. Arrange the greased "Crisper Basket" in the pot of Ninja Foodi Grill.
7. Close the Ninja Foodi Grill with lid and select "Air Crisp".
8. Set the temperature to 400 degrees F to preheat.
9. Press "Start/Stop" to begin preheating.
10. When the display shows "Add Food" open the lid and place the chops into the "Crisper Basket".
11. Close the Ninja Foodi Grill with lid and set the time for 15 minutes.
12. Press "Start/Stop" to begin cooking.
13. Flip the chops once halfway through.
14. When the cooking time is completed, press "Start/Stop" to stop cooking and open the lid.
15. Serve hot.

Nutritional Information per Serving:

Calories: 413 | Fat: 20.2g | Saturated Fat: 4.4g | Carbohydrates: 31g | Sugar: 0.1g | Protein: 28.3g

⏰ Prep Time 15 m | ⏱ Cooking Time 26 m | 4 Servings

Ingredients:

- ¼ cup honey, divided
- ¾ cup BBQ sauce
- 2 tablespoons tomato ketchup
- 1 tablespoon Worcestershire sauce
- 1 tablespoon soy sauce
- ½ teaspoon garlic powder
- Freshly ground white pepper, to taste
- 1¾ pounds pork ribs

Instructions:

1. In a bowl, mix together 3 tablespoons of honey and the remaining ingredients except pork ribs.
2. Add the pork ribs and coat with the mixture generously.
3. Refrigerate to marinate for about 20 minutes.
4. Arrange the greased "Crisper Basket" in the pot of Ninja Foodi Grill.
5. Close the Ninja Foodi Grill with lid and select "Air Crisp".
6. Set the temperature to 355 degrees F to preheat.
7. Press "Start/Stop" to begin preheating.
8. When the display shows "Add Food" open the lid and place the <u>pan</u> into the "Crisper Basket".
9. Close the Ninja Foodi Grill with lid and set the time for 26 minutes.
10. Press "Start/Stop" to begin cooking.
11. Flip the ribs once halfway through.
12. When the cooking time is completed, press "Start/Stop" to stop cooking and open the lid.
13. Transfer the ribs onto serving plates.
14. Drizzle with the remaining honey and serve immediately.

Nutritional Information per Serving:

Calories: 691 | Fat: 35.3 g | Saturated Fat: 12.5 g | Carbohydrates: 37 g | Sugar: 32.2 g | Protein: 53.1 g

⏰ Prep Time 15 m | ⏰ Cooking Time 20 m | 2 Servings

Ingredients:

- 2 (5-ounce) boneless pork chops
- 1 cup buttermilk
- ½ cup flour
- 1 teaspoon garlic powder
- Salt and freshly ground black pepper, to taste
- Olive oil cooking spray

Instructions:

1. In a bowl, place the chops and buttermilk and refrigerate, covered for about 12 hours.
2. Remove the chops from the bowl of buttermilk, discarding the buttermilk.
3. In a shallow dish, mix together the flour, garlic powder, salt, and black pepper.
4. Coat the chops with flour mixture generously.
5. Place the pork chops into a baking pan and spray with the cooking spray.
6. Arrange the "Crisper Basket" in the pot of Ninja Foodi Grill.
7. Close the Ninja Foodi Grill with lid and select "Air Crisp".
8. Set the temperature to 380 degrees F to preheat.
9. Press "Start/Stop" to begin preheating.
10. When the display shows "Add Food" open the lid and place the chops into the "Crisper Basket".
11. Close the Ninja Foodi Grill with lid and set the time for 20 minutes.
12. Press "Start/Stop" to begin cooking.
13. Flip the chops once halfway through.
14. When the cooking time is completed, press "Start/Stop" to stop cooking and open the lid.
15. Serve hot.

Nutritional Information per Serving:

Calories: 370 | Fat: 6.4g | Saturated Fat: 2.4g | Carbohydrates: 30.7g | Sugar: 6.3g | Protein: 44.6g

🕐 Prep Time 15 m | 🕐 Cooking Time 25 m | 4 Servings

Ingredients:

- 14 ounces lean ground pork
- 1 chorizo sausage, chopped finely
- 1 small onion, chopped
- 1 garlic clove, minced
- 2 tablespoons fresh cilantro, chopped
- 3 tablespoons breadcrumbs

- 1 egg
- Salt and freshly ground black pepper, to taste
- 2 tablespoons fresh mushrooms, sliced thinly
- 2 tablespoons olive oil

Instructions:

1. In a large bowl, add all ingredients except for mushrooms and mix until well combined.
2. In a baking pan, place the pork mixture and with the back of a spatula, smooth the surface.
3. Top with mushroom slices and gently press into the meatloaf.
4. Drizzle with oil evenly.
5. Arrange the "Crisper Basket" in the pot of Ninja Foodi Grill.
6. Close the Ninja Foodi Grill with lid and select "Air Crisp".
7. Set the temperature to 390 degrees F to preheat.
8. Press "Start/Stop" to begin preheating.
9. When the display shows "Add Food" open the lid and place the pan into the "Crisper Basket".
10. Close the Ninja Foodi Grill with lid and set the time for 25 minutes.
11. Press "Start/Stop" to begin cooking.
12. When cooking time is completed, press "Start/Stop" to stop cooking and open the lid.
13. Cut the meatloaf into desired sized slices and serve.

Nutritional Information per Serving:

Calories: 301 | Fat: 16.5g | Saturated Fat: 4.1g | Carbohydrates: 5.7g | Sugar: 1.2g | Protein: 31.5g

⏱ Prep Time 15 m | ⏱ Cooking Time 15 m | 4 Servings

Ingredients:

- 4 garlic cloves, crushed
- 1 tablespoon fresh lemon juice
- 1 teaspoon olive oil
- 1 tablespoon Za'atar

- Salt and freshly ground black pepper, to taste
- 8 (3½-ounces) bone-in lamb loin chops, trimmed

Instructions:

1. In a large bowl, mix together the garlic, lemon juice, oil, Za'atar, salt and black pepper.
2. Coat the chops with the garlic mixture.
3. Arrange the greased "Crisper Basket" in the pot of Ninja Foodi Grill.
4. Close the Ninja Foodi Grill with lid and select "Air Crisp".
5. Set the temperature to 400 degrees F to preheat.
6. Press "Start/Stop" to begin preheating.
7. When the display shows "Add Food" open the lid and place the chops into the "Crisper Basket".
8. Close the Ninja Foodi Grill with lid and set the time for 15 minutes.
9. Press "Start/Stop" to begin cooking.
10. Flip the chops once halfway through.
11. When the cooking time is completed, press "Start/Stop" to stop cooking and open the lid.
12. Serve hot.

Nutritional Information per Serving:

Calories: 385 | Fat: 15.8g | Saturated Fat: 5.4g | Carbohydrates: 1.1g | Sugar: 0.1g | Protein: 55.9g

🕐 Prep Time 15 m | 🕐 Cooking Time 15 m | 2 Servings

Ingredients:

- 1 tablespoon Dijon mustard
- ½ tablespoon fresh lemon juice
- ½ teaspoon olive oil
- ½ teaspoon dried tarragon
- Salt and freshly ground black pepper, to taste
- 4 (4-ounce) lamb loin chops

Instructions:

1. In a large bowl, mix together the mustard, lemon juice, oil, tarragon, salt, and black pepper.
2. Add the chops and generously coat with the mixture.
3. Arrange the greased "Crisper Basket" in the pot of Ninja Foodi Grill.
4. Close the Ninja Foodi Grill with lid and select "Air Crisp".
5. Set the temperature to 390 degrees F to preheat.
6. Press "Start/Stop" to begin preheating.
7. When the display shows "Add Food" open the lid and place the lamb chops into the "Crisper Basket".
8. Close the Ninja Foodi Grill with lid and set the time for 15 minutes.
9. Press "Start/Stop" to begin cooking.
10. Flip the chops once halfway through.
11. When the cooking time is completed, press "Start/Stop" to stop cooking and open the lid.
12. Serve hot.

Nutritional Information per Serving:

Calories: 438 | Fat: 18.1g | Saturated Fat: 6.2g | Carbohydrates: 0.6g | Sugar: 0.2g | Protein: 64.1g

⏱ Prep Time 15 m | ⏱ Cooking Time 6 m | 2 Servings

Ingredients:

- 1 tablespoon olive oil, divided
- 2 garlic cloves, minced
- 1 tablespoon fresh rosemary, chopped
- Salt and freshly ground black pepper, to taste
- 4 (4-ounce) lamb chops

Instructions:

1. In a large bowl, mix together the oil, garlic, rosemary, salt and black pepper.
2. Coat the chops with half of the garlic mixture.
3. Arrange the greased "Crisper Basket" in the pot of Ninja Foodi Grill.
4. Close the Ninja Foodi Grill with lid and select "Air Crisp".
5. Set the temperature to 390 degrees F to preheat.
6. Press "Start/Stop" to begin preheating.
7. When the display shows "Add Food" open the lid and place the lamb chops into the "Crisper Basket".
8. Close the Ninja Foodi Grill with lid and set the time for 6 minutes.
9. Press "Start/Stop" to begin cooking.
10. Flip the chops once halfway through.
11. When the cooking time is completed, press "Start/Stop" to stop cooking and open the lid.
12. Transfer the chops onto a platter and top with the remaining garlic mixture.
13. Serve hot

Nutritional Information per Serving:

Calories: 492 | Fat: 23.9g | Saturated Fat: 7.1g | Carbohydrates: 2.1g | Sugar: 0g | Protein: 64g

⏰ Prep Time 10 m | ⏰ Cooking Time 7 m | 2 Servings

Ingredients:

- 1 tablespoon fresh lemon juice
- 1 tablespoon olive oil
- 1 teaspoon dried rosemary
- 1 teaspoon dried thyme
- 1 teaspoon dried oregano
- ½ teaspoon ground cumin
- ½ teaspoon ground coriander
- Salt and freshly ground black pepper, to taste
- 4 (4-ounces) lamb chops

Instructions:

1. In a large bowl, mix together the lemon juice, oil, herbs, and spices.
2. Add the chops and coat evenly with the herb mixture.
3. Refrigerate to marinate for about 1 hour.
4. Arrange the greased "Crisper Basket" in the pot of Ninja Foodi Grill.
5. Close the Ninja Foodi Grill with lid and select "Air Crisp".
6. Set the temperature to 390 degrees F to preheat.
7. Press "Start/Stop" to begin preheating.
8. When the display shows "Add Food" open the lid and place the lamb chops into the "Crisper Basket".
9. Close the Ninja Foodi Grill with lid and set the time for 7 minutes.
10. Press "Start/Stop" to begin cooking.
11. Flip the chops once halfway through.
12. When the cooking time is completed, press "Start/Stop" to stop cooking and open the lid.
13. Transfer the chops onto a platter and top with the remaining garlic mixture.
14. Serve hot

Nutritional Information per Serving:

Calories: 491 | Fat: 24g | Saturated Fat: 7.1g | Carbohydrates: 1.9g | Sugar: 0.2g | Protein: 64g

⏰ Prep Time 15 m | ⏰ Cooking Time 30 m | 5 Servings

Ingredients:

- 1 tablespoon butter, melted
- 1 garlic clove, chopped finely
- Salt and freshly ground black pepper, to taste
- 1 (1¾-pound) rack of lamb

- 1 egg
- ½ cup panko breadcrumbs
- 1 tablespoon fresh thyme, minced
- 1 tablespoon fresh rosemary, minced

Instructions:

1. In a bowl, mix together the butter, garlic, salt, and black pepper.
2. Coat the rack of lamb with garlic mixture generously.
3. In a shallow dish, beat the egg.
4. In another dish, mix together the breadcrumbs and herbs.
5. Dip the rack of lamb in beaten egg and then coat with breadcrumbs mixture.
6. Arrange the "Crisper Basket" in the pot of Ninja Foodi Grill.
7. Close the Ninja Foodi Grill with lid and select "Air Crisp".
8. Set the temperature to 215 degrees F to preheat.
9. Press "Start/Stop" to begin preheating.
10. When the display shows "Add Food" open the lid and place the rack of lamb into the "Crisper Basket".
11. Close the Ninja Foodi Grill with lid and set the time for 25 minutes.
12. Press "Start/Stop" to begin cooking.
13. After 25 minutes of cooking, set the temperature to 390 degrees F for 5 minutes.
14. When the cooking time is completed, press "Start/Stop" to stop cooking and open the lid.
15. Place the rack of lamb onto a cutting board for about 10 minutes.
16. Cut the rack into individual chops and serve.

Nutritional Information per Serving:

Calories: 343 | Fat: 18.1g | Saturated Fat: 7g | Carbohydrates: 0.1g | Sugar: 2.7g | Protein: 33.9g

⏱ Prep Time 10 m | ⏱ Cooking Time 1 h 15 m | 6 Servings

Ingredients:

- 1 (2¼-pound) boneless leg of lamb
- 2 tablespoons olive oil
- Salt and freshly ground black pepper, to taste

- 2 fresh rosemary sprigs
- 2 fresh thyme sprigs

Instructions:

1. Coat the leg of lamb with oil and sprinkle with salt and black pepper.
2. Wrap the leg of lamb with herb sprigs.
3. Arrange the "Crisper Basket" in the pot of Ninja Foodi Grill.
4. Close the Ninja Foodi Grill with lid and select "Air Crisp".
5. Set the temperature to 300 degrees F to preheat.
6. Press "Start/Stop" to begin preheating.
7. When the display shows "Add Food" open the lid and place the leg of lamb into the "Crisper Basket".
8. Close the Ninja Foodi Grill with lid and set the time for 75 minutes.
9. Press "Start/Stop" to begin cooking.
10. When the cooking time is completed, press "Start/Stop" to stop cooking and open the lid.
11. Transfer the leg of lamb onto a cutting board for about 10 minutes before slicing.
12. Cut into desired sized pieces and serve.

Nutritional Information per Serving:

Calories: 360 | Fat: 17.3g | Saturated Fat: 5. g | Carbohydrates: 0.7 g | Sugar: 0g | Protein: 47.8g

⏰ Prep Time 20 m | ⏰ Cooking Time 30 m | 8 Servings

Ingredients:
For Meatballs:

- 2 pounds lean ground lamb
- 2/3 cup quick-cooking oats
- ½ cup Ritz crackers, crushed
- 1 (5-ounce) can evaporated milk
- 2 large eggs, beaten lightly
- 1 teaspoon honey
- 1 tablespoon dried onion, minced
- 1 teaspoon garlic powder
- 1 teaspoon ground cumin

- Salt and freshly ground black pepper, to taste

For Sauce:

- 1/3 cup orange marmalade
- 1/3 cup honey
- 1/3 cup brown sugar
- 2 tablespoons cornstarch
- 2 tablespoons soy sauce
- 1-2 tablespoons hot sauce
- 1 tablespoon Worcestershire sauce

Instructions:

1. For meatballs: in a large bowl, add all the ingredients and mix until well combined.
2. Make 1½-inch balls from the mixture.
3. Arrange the meatballs onto a baking pan in a single layer.
4. Arrange the "Crisper Basket" in the pot of Ninja Foodi Grill.
5. Close the Ninja Foodi Grill with lid and select "Air Crisp".
6. Set the temperature to 380 degrees F to preheat.
7. Press "Start/Stop" to begin preheating.
8. When the display shows "Add Food" open the lid and place the pan into the "Crisper Basket".
9. Close the Ninja Foodi Grill with lid and set the time for 15 minutes.
10. Press "Start/Stop" to begin cooking.
11. Flip the meatballs once halfway through.
12. Meanwhile, for sauce: in a small pan, add all the ingredients over medium heat and cook until thickened, stirring continuously.
13. When the cooking time is completed, press "Start/Stop" to stop cooking and open the lid.
14. Serve the meatballs with the topping of sauce.

Nutritional Information per Serving:

Calories: 413 | Fat: 11.9g | Saturated Fat: 4.3g | Carbohydrates: 39.5g | Sugar: 28.2g | Protein: 36.2g

⏰ Prep Time 10 m | ⏰ Cooking Time 13 m | 2 Servings

Ingredients:

- 3 tablespoons low-sodium soy sauce
- 2 tablespoons maple syrup
- 2 teaspoons fresh lemon juice
- 2 teaspoons water
- 2 (4-ounce) salmon fillets

Instructions:

1. Place all the ingredients in a small bowl except the salmon and mix well.
2. In a small bowl, reserve about half of the mixture.
3. Add the salmon in the remaining mixture and coat well.
4. Refrigerate, covered to marinate for about 2 hours.
5. Arrange the "Crisper Basket" in the pot of Ninja Foodi Grill
6. Close the Ninja Foodi Grill with lid and select "Air Crisp".
7. Set the temperature to 355 degrees F to preheat.
8. Press "Start/Stop" to begin preheating.
9. When the display shows "Add Food" open the lid and place the salmon fillets into the "Crisper Basket" in a single layer.
10. Close the Ninja Foodi Grill with lid and set the time for 13 minutes.
11. Press "Start/Stop" to begin cooking.
12. After 8 minutes, flip the salmon fillets and coat with reserved marinade.
13. When the cooking time is completed, press "Start/Stop" to stop cooking and open the lid.
14. Serve hot.

Nutritional Information per Serving:

Calories: 211 | Fat: 7.1g | Saturated Fat: 1.1g | Carbohydrates: 15g | Sugar: 13.5g | Protein: 23.5g

⏰ Prep Time 15 m | ⏱ Cooking Time 15 m | 2 Servings

Ingredients:

- 2 (6-ounce) skinless salmon fillets
- Salt and freshly ground black pepper, to taste
- 3 tablespoons walnuts, chopped finely
- 3 tablespoons quick-cooking oats, crushed
- 2 tablespoons olive oil

Instructions:

1. Rub the salmon fillets with salt and black pepper evenly.
2. In a bowl, mix together the walnuts, oats and oil.
3. Arrange the salmon fillets into the greased baking pan in a single layer.
4. Place the oat mixture over salmon fillets and gently press down.
5. Arrange the "Crisper Basket" in the pot of Ninja Foodi Grill.
6. Close the Ninja Foodi Grill with lid and select "Bake".
7. Set the temperature to 400 degrees F to preheat.
8. Press "Start/Stop" to begin preheating.
9. When the display shows "Add Food" open the lid and place the <u>pan</u> into the "Crisper Basket".
10. Close the Ninja Foodi Grill with lid and set the time for 15 minutes.
11. Press "Start/Stop" to begin cooking.
12. When the cooking time is completed, press "Start/Stop" to stop cooking and open the lid.
13. Serve hot.

Nutritional Information per Serving:

Calories: 446 | Fat: 31.9g | Saturated Fat: 4g | Carbohydrates: 6.4g | Sugar: 0.2g | Protein: 36.8g

⏰ Prep Time 10 m | ⏰ Cooking Time 10 m | 2 Servings

Ingredients:

- 2 (6-ounces) trout fillets
- Salt and freshly ground black pepper, to taste
- 1 tablespoon butter, melted

Instructions:

1. Season each trout fillet with salt and black pepper and then coat with the butter.
2. Arrange the trout fillets into q greased baking pan in a single layer.
3. Arrange the "Crisper Basket" in the pot of Ninja Foodi Grill.
4. Close the Ninja Foodi Grill with lid and select "Air Crisp".
5. Set the temperature to 360 degrees F to preheat.
6. Press "Start/Stop" to begin preheating.
7. When the display shows "Add Food" open the lid and place the pan into the "Crisper Basket".
8. Close the Ninja Foodi Grill with lid and set the time for 10 minutes.
9. Press "Start/Stop" to begin cooking.
10. Flip the fillets once halfway through.
11. When the cooking time is completed, press "Start/Stop" to stop cooking and open the lid.
12. Serve hot.

Nutritional Information per Serving:

Calories: 374 | Fat: 20.2g | Saturated Fat: 6.2g | Carbohydrates: 0g | Sugar: 0g | Protein: 45.4g

⏰ Prep Time 10 m | ⏰ Cooking Time 10 m | 2 Servings

Ingredients:

- 1 tablespoon fresh lime juice
- ½ tablespoons olive oil
- Salt and freshly ground black pepper, to taste
- 1 garlic clove, minced
- ½ teaspoon fresh thyme leaves, chopped
- ½ teaspoon fresh rosemary, chopped
- 2 (7-ounce) halibut fillets

Instructions:

1. In a bowl, add all the ingredients except the halibut fillets and mix well.
2. Add the halibut fillets and coat with the mixture generously.
3. Arrange the "Crisper Basket" in the pot of Ninja Foodi Grill.
4. Close the Ninja Foodi Grill with lid and select "Bake".
5. Set the temperature to 400 degrees F to preheat.
6. Press "Start/Stop" to begin preheating.
7. When the display shows "Add Food" open the lid and place the halibut fillets into the "Crisper Basket".
8. Close the Ninja Foodi Grill with lid and set the time for 10 minutes.
9. Press "Start/Stop" to begin cooking.
10. Flip the fillets once halfway through.
11. When the cooking time is completed, press "Start/Stop" to stop cooking and open the lid.
12. Serve hot.

Nutritional Information per Serving:

Calories: 255 | Fat: 8.2g | Saturated Fat: 1.1g | Carbohydrates: 0.9g | Sugar: 0g | Protein: 41.9g

⏰ Prep Time 15 m | ⏰ Cooking Time 15 m | 4 Servings

Ingredients:

- 4 (4-ounce) (¾-inch thick) cod fillets
- Salt, to taste
- 2 tablespoons all-purpose flour
- 2 eggs
- ½ cup panko breadcrumbs
- 1 teaspoon fresh dill, minced

- ½ teaspoon dry mustard
- ½ teaspoon lemon zest, grated
- ½ teaspoon onion powder
- ½ teaspoon paprika
- Olive oil cooking spray

Instructions:

1. Season the cod fillets with salt pepper generously.
2. In a shallow bowl, place the flour.
3. Crack the eggs in a second bowl and beat well.
4. In a third bowl, mix together the panko, dill, lemon zest, mustard and spices.
5. Coat each cod fillet with the flour, then dip into beaten eggs and finally, coat with panko mixture.
6. Arrange the greased "Crisper Basket" in the pot of Ninja Foodi Grill.
7. Close the Ninja Foodi Grill with lid and select "Air Crisp".
8. Set the temperature to 400 degrees F to preheat.
9. Press "Start/Stop" to begin preheating.
10. When the display shows "Add Food" open the lid and place the cod fillets into the "Crisper Basket".
11. Spray the cod fillets with cooking spray.
12. Close the Ninja Foodi Grill with lid and set the time for 15 minutes.
13. Press "Start/Stop" to begin cooking.
14. While cooking, flip the cod fillets once halfway through and spray with cooking spray.
15. When the cooking time is completed, press "Start/Stop" to stop cooking and open the lid.
16. Serve hot.

Nutritional Information per Serving:

Calories: 190 | Fat: 4.3g | Saturated Fat: 1.1g | Carbohydrates: 5.9 g | Sugar: 0.4g | Protein: 24g

⏰ Prep Time 0 m | ⏰ Cooking Time 12 m | 2 Servings

Ingredients:

- ½ teaspoon lemon pepper seasoning
- ½ teaspoon garlic powder
- 1/2 teaspoon onion powder
- Salt and freshly ground black pepper, to taste
- 2 (6-ounce) tilapia fillets
- 1 tablespoon olive oil

Instructions:

1. In a small bowl, mix together the spices, salt and black pepper.
2. Coat the tilapia fillets with oil and then rub with spice mixture.
3. Arrange the greased "Crisper Basket" in the pot of Ninja Foodi Grill.
4. Close the Ninja Foodi Grill with lid and select "Air Crisp".
5. Set the temperature to 360 degrees F to preheat.
6. Press "Start/Stop" to begin preheating.
7. When the display shows "Add Food" open the lid and place the tilapia fillets into the "Crisper Basket".
8. Close the Ninja Foodi Grill with lid and set the time for 12 minutes.
9. Press "Start/Stop" to begin cooking.
10. Flip the fillets once halfway through.
11. When the cooking time is completed, press "Start/Stop" to stop cooking and open the lid.
12. Serve hot.

Nutritional Information per Serving:

Calories: 206 | Fat: 8.6g | Saturated Fat: 1.7g | Carbohydrates: 1.3g | Sugar: 0.4g | Protein: 31.9g

⏰ Prep Time 10 m | ⏰ Cooking Time 20 m | 4 Servings

Ingredients:

- 4 (4-ounce) catfish fillets
- ¼ cup Louisiana fish fry seasoning
- 1 tablespoon olive oil
- 1 tablespoon fresh parsley, chopped

Instructions:

1. Rub the fish fillets with seasoning generously and then, coat with oil.
2. Arrange the greased "Crisper Basket" in the pot of Ninja Foodi Grill.
3. Close the Ninja Foodi Grill with lid and select "Air Crisp".
4. Set the temperature to 400 degrees F to preheat.
5. Press "Start/Stop" to begin preheating.
6. When the display shows "Add Food" open the lid and place the fish fillets into the "Crisper Basket".
7. Close the Ninja Foodi Grill with lid and set the time for 20 minutes.
8. Press "Start/Stop" to begin cooking.
9. After 10 minutes of cooking, flip the fish fillets.
10. When the cooking time is completed, press "Start/Stop" to stop cooking and open the lid.
11. Serve hot with the garnishing of parsley.

Nutritional Information per Serving:

Calories: 213 | Fat: 12.1g | Saturated Fat: 2.1g | Carbohydrates: 7.6g | Sugar: 0g | Protein: 17.7g

⏰ Prep Time 15 m | ⏰ Cooking Time 20 m | 4 Servings

Ingredients:

- 2/3 cup Parmesan cheese, grated
- 4 garlic cloves, minced
- 2 tablespoons olive oil
- 1 teaspoon dried basil
- ½ teaspoon dried oregano
- 1 teaspoon onion powder
- ½ teaspoon red pepper flakes, crushed
- Freshly ground black pepper, to taste
- 2 pounds shrimp, peeled and deveined
- 1-2 tablespoons fresh lemon juice

Instructions:

1. In a large bowl, add the Parmesan cheese, garlic, oil, herbs, and spices and mix well
2. Add the shrimp and toss to coat well.
3. Arrange the greased "Crisper Basket" in the pot of Ninja Foodi Grill.
4. Close the Ninja Foodi Grill with lid and select "Air Crisp".
5. Set the temperature to 350 degrees F to preheat.
6. Press "Start/Stop" to begin preheating.
7. When the display shows "Add Food" open the lid and place half of the shrimp into the "Crisper Basket" in a single layer.
8. Close the Ninja Foodi Grill with lid and set the time for 10 minutes.
9. Press "Start/Stop" to begin cooking.
10. When the cooking time is completed, press "Start/Stop" to stop cooking and open the lid.
11. Transfer the shrimp onto a platter.
12. Repeat with the remaining shrimp.
13. Drizzle with lemon juice and serve immediately.

Nutritional Information per Serving:

Calories: 386 | Fat: 14.2g | Saturated Fat: 3.8g | Carbohydrates: 5. g | Sugar: 0.4g | Protein: 57.3g

🕐 Prep Time 15 m | 🕐 Cooking Time 6 m | 6 Servings

Ingredients:

- ½ cup butter
- 4 garlic cloves, minced
- 1 tablespoon fresh rosemary, chopped
- 1 tablespoon fresh thyme, chopped
- 2 pounds sea scallops
- Salt and freshly ground black pepper, to taste

Instructions:

1. In a skillet, melt the butter over medium heat and sauté the garlic and rosemary for about 1 minute.
2. Stir in the scallops, salt and black pepper and cook for about 2 minutes.
3. Remove from the heat and place the scallop mixture into a baking pan..
4. Arrange the greased "Crisper Basket" in the pot of Ninja Foodi Grill.
5. Close the Ninja Foodi Grill with lid and select "Air Crisp".
6. Set the temperature to 350 degrees F to preheat.
7. Press "Start/Stop" to begin preheating.
8. When the display shows "Add Food" open the lid and place the pan into the "Crisper Basket".
9. Close the Ninja Foodi Grill with lid and set the time for 3 minutes.
10. Press "Start/Stop" to begin cooking.
11. When cooking time is completed, press "Start/Stop" to stop cooking and open the lid.
12. Serve hot.

Nutritional Information per Serving:

Calories: 275 | Fat: 16.6g | Saturated Fat: 9.9g | Carbohydrates: 4.9g | Sugar: 0g | Protein: 25.7g

⏰ Prep Time 15 m | ⏱ Cooking Time 13 m | 3 Servings

Ingredients:

- ¾ pound calamari tubes, washed and cut into ¼-inch rings
- 1 cup club soda
- 1 cup flour
- ½ tablespoon red pepper flakes, crushed
- Salt and freshly ground black pepper, to taste
- 2 tablespoons Sriracha
- ½ cup honey
- Olive oil cooking spray

Instructions:

1. In a large bowl, place the calamari and club soda and set aside for about 10 minutes.
2. Meanwhile, in a shallow bowl, place the flour, red pepper flakes, salt and black pepper and mix well.
3. Drain the club soda from the calamari.
4. With the paper towels, pat dry the calamari rings.
5. Coat the calamari rings with flour mixture evenly.
6. Arrange the greased "Crisper Basket" in the pot of Ninja Foodi Grill.
7. Close the Ninja Foodi Grill with lid and select "Air Crisp".
8. Set the temperature to 375 degrees F to preheat.
9. Press "Start/Stop" to begin preheating.
10. When the display shows "Add Food" open the lid and place the calamari rings into the "Crisper Basket".
11. Close the Ninja Foodi Grill with lid and set the time for 13 minutes.
12. Press "Start/Stop" to begin cooking.
13. While cooking, shake the "Crisper Basket" occasionally.
14. Meanwhile, in a bowl, place the Sriracha and honey and beat until well combined.
15. After 11 minutes, coat the calamari rings with honey mixture evenly.
16. When cooking time is completed, press "Start/Stop" to stop cooking and open the lid.
17. Serve hot.

Nutritional Information per Serving:

Calories: 336 | Fat: 4.6g | Saturated Fat: 0.6g | Carbohydrates: 89.4g | Sugar: 46.6g | Protein: 12.6g

⏰ Prep Time 15 m | ⏰ Cooking Time 18 m | 5 Servings

Ingredients:

- 1 tablespoon olive oil
- 1 tablespoon garlic, minced
- 1 cup cauliflower florets
- 1 cup broccoli florets
- 1 cup zucchini, sliced
- ½ cup yellow squash, sliced
- ½ cup fresh mushrooms, sliced
- 1 small onion, sliced
- ¼ cup balsamic vinegar
- 1 teaspoon red pepper flakes
- Salt and freshly ground black pepper, to taste
- ¼ cup Parmesan cheese, grated

Instructions:

1. In a large bowl, add all the ingredients except or cheese and toss to coat well.
2. Arrange the greased "Crisper Basket" in the pot of Ninja Foodi
3. Close the Ninja Foodi Grill with lid and select "Air Crisp".
4. Set the temperature to 400 degrees F to preheat.
5. Press "Start/Stop" to begin preheating.
6. When the display shows "Add Food" open the lid and place the vegetables into the "Crisper Basket".
7. Close the Ninja Foodi Grill with lid and set the time for 18 minutes.
8. Press "Start/Stop" to begin cooking.
9. After 8 minutes of cooking, flip the vegetables and sprinkle with cheese evenly.
10. When the cooking time is completed, press "Start/Stop" to stop cooking and open the lid.
11. Serve hot.

Nutritional Information per Serving:

Calories: 68 | Fat: 4g | Saturated Fat: 0.9g | Carbohydrates: 5.8g | Sugar: 2.2g | Protein: 3.4 g

⏰ Prep Time 15 m | ⏰ Cooking Time 25 m | 4 Servings

Ingredients:

- 2 ounces cherry tomatoes
- 2 large zucchini, chopped
- 2 green bell peppers, seeded and chopped
- 6 tablespoons olive oil, divided
- 2 tablespoons honey
- 1 teaspoon Dijon mustard
- 1 teaspoon dried herbs
- 1 teaspoon garlic paste
- Salt, to taste

Instructions:

1. In a parchment paper-lined baking pan, place the vegetables and drizzle with 3 tablespoons of oil.
2. Arrange the "Crisper Basket" in the pot of Ninja Foodi Grill.
3. Close the Ninja Foodi Grill with lid and select "Air Crisp".
4. Set the temperature to 350 degrees F to preheat.
5. Press "Start/Stop" to begin preheating.
6. When the display shows "Add Food" open the lid and place the pan into the "Crisper Basket".
7. Close the Ninja Foodi Grill with lid and set the time for 20 minutes.
8. Press "Start/Stop" to begin cooking.
9. Meanwhile, in a bowl, add the remaining oil, honey, mustard, herbs, garlic, salt, and black pepper and mix well.
10. When the cooking time is completed, press "Start/Stop" to stop cooking and open the lid.
11. Stir the honey mixture with vegetable mixture.
12. Again, arrange the pan into the "Crisper Basket".
13. Close the Ninja Foodi Grill with lid and set the temperature to 392 degrees F for 5 minutes.
14. Press "Start/Stop" to begin cooking.
15. When the cooking time is completed, press "Start/Stop" to stop cooking and open the lid.
16. Serve immediately.

Nutritional Information per Serving:

Calories: 262 | Fat: 21.5g | Saturated Fat: 3.1g | Carbohydrates: 19.5g | Sugar: 14.8g | Protein: 2.8g

🕐 Prep Time 15 m | 🕐 Cooking Time 20 m | 4 Servings

Ingredients:

- 2 large potatoes, sliced thinly
- 5½ tablespoons cream
- 2 eggs
- 1 tablespoon plain flour
- ½ cup cheddar cheese, grated

Instructions:

1. Arrange the "Crisper Basket" in the pot of Ninja Foodi Grill.
2. Close the Ninja Foodi Grill with lid and select "Air Crisp".
3. Set the temperature to 355 degrees F to preheat.
4. Press "Start/Stop" to begin preheating.
5. When the display shows "Add Food" open the lid and place the potato slices into the "Crisper Basket".
6. Close the Ninja Foodi Grill with lid and set the time for 10 minutes.
7. Press "Start/Stop" to begin cooking.
8. Meanwhile, in a bowl, add cream, eggs and flour and mix until a thick sauce forms.
9. When the cooking time is completed, press "Start/Stop" to stop cooking and open the lid.
10. Remove the potato slices from the "Crisper Basket".
11. Divide the potato slices in 4 ramekins evenly and top with the egg mixture evenly, followed by the cheese.
12. Arrange the ramekins into the "Crisper Basket".
13. Close the Ninja Foodi Grill with lid and select "Air Crisp".
14. Set the temperature to 390 degrees F for 10 minutes.
15. Press "Start/Stop" to begin cooking.
16. When the cooking time is completed, press "Start/Stop" to stop cooking and open the lid.
17. Serve warm.

Nutritional Information per Serving:

Calories: 233 | Fat: 8g | Saturated Fat: 4.3g | Carbohydrates: 31.3 g | Sugar: 2.7g | Protein: 9.7g

🕐 Prep Time 35 m | 🕐 Cooking Time 15 m | 4 Servings

Ingredients:

- 2 zucchinis, cut in half lengthwise
- ½ teaspoon garlic powder
- Salt, to taste
- 1 teaspoon olive oil
- 4 ounces fresh mushrooms, chopped
- 4 ounces carrots, peeled and shredded
- 3 ounces onion, chopped
- 4 ounces goat cheese, crumbled
- 12 fresh basil leaves
- ½ teaspoon onion powder

Instructions:

1. Carefully scoop the flesh from the middle of each zucchini half.
2. Season each zucchini half with a little garlic powder and salt.
3. Arrange the zucchini halves into the greased baking pan.
4. Place the oat mixture over salmon fillets and gently press down.
5. Arrange the "Crisper Basket" in the pot of Ninja Foodi Grill.
6. Close the Ninja Foodi Grill with lid and select "Bake".
7. Set the temperature to 450 degrees F to preheat.
8. Press "Start/Stop" to begin preheating.
9. When the display shows "Add Food" open the lid and place the pan into the "Crisper Basket".
10. Close the Ninja Foodi Grill with lid and set the time for 20 minutes.
11. Press "Start/Stop" to begin cooking.
12. Meanwhile, in a skillet, heat the oil over medium heat and cook the mushrooms, carrots, onions, onion powder and salt and cook for about 5-6 minutes.
13. Remove from the heat and set aside.
14. When the cooking time is completed, press "Start/Stop" to stop cooking and open the lid.
15. Stuff each zucchini half with veggie mixture and top with basil leaves, followed by the cheese.
16. Close the Ninja Foodi Grill with lid and select "Bake".
17. Set the temperature to 450 degrees F for 15 minutes.
18. When the cooking time is completed, press "Start/Stop" to stop cooking and open the lid.
19. Serve warm.

Nutritional Information per Serving:

Calories: 181 | Fat: 11.6g | Saturated Fat: 7.2g | Carbohydrates: 10.1g | Sugar: 5.3g | Protein: 11.3g

⏰ Prep Time 15 m | ⏰ Cooking Time 12 m | 6 Servings

Ingredients:

- 24 ounces fresh green beans, trimmed
- 2 cups fresh button mushrooms, sliced
- 3 tablespoons olive oil
- 2 tablespoons fresh lemon juice
- 1 teaspoon ground sage
- 1 teaspoon garlic powder
- 1 teaspoon onion powder
- Salt and freshly ground black pepper, to taste
- 1/3 cup French fried onions

Instructions:

1. In a bowl, add the green beans, mushrooms, oil, lemon juice, sage, and spices and toss to coat well.
2. Arrange the greased "Crisper Basket" in the pot of Ninja Foodi Grill.
3. Close the Ninja Foodi Grill with lid and select "Air Crisp".
4. Set the temperature to 400 degrees F to preheat.
5. Press "Start/Stop" to begin preheating.
6. When the display shows "Add Food" open the lid and place the mushroom mixture into the "Crisper Basket".
7. Close the Ninja Foodi Grill with lid and set the time for 12 minutes.
8. Press "Start/Stop" to begin cooking.
9. While cooking, shake the mushroom mixture occasionally.
10. When the cooking time is completed, press "Start/Stop" to stop cooking and open the lid.
11. Transfer the mushroom mixture into a serving dish.
12. Top with fried onions and serve.

Nutritional Information per Serving:

Calories: 125 | Fat: 8.6g | Saturated Fat: 2g | Carbohydrates: 11g | Sugar: 2.4g | Protein: 3g

⏰ Prep Time 15 m | ⏰ Cooking Time 15 m | 3 Servings

Ingredients:

- 8 ounces firm tofu, drained, pressed and cubed
- 1 head broccoli, cut into florets
- 1 tablespoon butter, melted
- 1 teaspoon ground turmeric
- ¼ teaspoon paprika
- Salt and freshly ground black pepper, to taste

Instructions:

1. In a bowl, mix together all ingredients.
2. Place the tofu mixture in the greased cooking pan.
3. Arrange the "Crisper Basket" in the pot of Ninja Foodi Grill.
4. Close the Ninja Foodi Grill with lid and select "Air Crisp".
5. Set the temperature to 390 degrees F to preheat.
6. Press "Start/Stop" to begin preheating.
7. When the display shows "Add Food" open the lid and place the pan into the "Crisper Basket".
8. Close the Ninja Foodi Grill with lid and set the time for 15 minutes.
9. Press "Start/Stop" to begin cooking.
10. Toss the tofu mixture once halfway through.
11. When the cooking time is completed, press "Start/Stop" to stop cooking and open the lid.
12. Serve hot.

Nutritional Information per Serving:

Calories: 119 | Fat: 7.4g | Saturated Fat: 3.1g | Carbohydrates: 7.5g | Sugar: 1.9g | Protein: 8.7g

⏰ Prep Time 15 m | ⏱ Cooking Time 18 m | 2 Servings

Ingredients:

- 2 cups cooked white rice
- 1 tablespoon vegetable oil
- 2 teaspoons sesame oil, toasted and divided
- 1 tablespoon water
- Salt and freshly ground white pepper, to taste
- 1 large egg, lightly beaten
- ½ cup frozen peas, thawed
- ½ cup frozen carrots, thawed
- 1 teaspoon soy sauce
- 1 teaspoon Sriracha sauce
- ½ teaspoon sesame seeds, toasted

Instructions:

1. In a large bowl, add the rice, vegetable oil, one teaspoon of sesame oil, water, salt, and white pepper and mix well.
2. Transfer rice mixture into a greased baking pan.
3. Arrange the "Crisper Basket" in the pot of Ninja Foodi Grill.
4. Close the Ninja Foodi Grill with lid and select "Air Crisp".
5. Set the temperature to 380 degrees F to preheat.
6. Press "Start/Stop" to begin preheating.
7. When the display shows "Add Food" open the lid and place the pan into the "Crisper Basket".
8. Close the Ninja Foodi Grill with lid and set the time for 18 minutes.
9. Press "Start/Stop" to begin cooking.
10. While cooking, stir the mixture once after 12 minutes.
11. After 12 minutes of cooking, place the beaten egg over rice.
12. After 16 minutes of cooking, stir in the peas and carrots.
13. Meanwhile, in a bowl, mix together the soy sauce, Sriracha sauce, sesame seeds and the remaining sesame oil.
14. When the cooking time is completed, press "Start/Stop" to stop cooking and open the lid.
15. transfer the rice mixture into a serving bowl
16. Drizzle with the sauce mixture and serve.

Nutritional Information per Serving:

Calories: 443 | Fat: 16.4g | Saturated Fat: 3.2g | Carbohydrates: 63.2g | Sugar: 3.6g | Protein: 10.1g

⏰ Prep Time 15 m | ⏰ Cooking Time 12 m | 3 Servings

Ingredients:

- 3 tablespoons white flour
- 2 eggs
- 3 tablespoons milk
- ½ cup plain breadcrumbs
- ½ pound mozzarella cheese block, cut into 3x½-inch sticks

Instructions:

1. In a shallow dish, place the flour.
2. In a second shallow dish, add eggs and milk and beat well.
3. In a third shallow dish, place the breadcrumbs.
4. Coat the Mozzarella sticks with flour, then dip into egg mixture and finally, coat with the breadcrumbs.
5. Arrange the Mozzarella sticks onto a cookie sheet and freeze for about 1-2 hours.
6. Arrange the "Crisper Basket" in the pot of Ninja Foodi Grill.
7. Close the Ninja Foodi Grill with lid and select "Air Crisp".
8. Set the temperature to 400 degrees F to preheat.
9. Press "Start/Stop" to begin preheating.
10. When the display shows "Add Food" open the lid and place the mozzarella sticks into the "Crisper Basket".
11. Close the Ninja Foodi Grill with lid and set the time for 12 minutes.
12. Press "Start/Stop" to begin cooking.
13. When the cooking time is completed, press "Start/Stop" to stop cooking and open the lid.
14. Serve warm.

Nutritional Information per Serving:

Calories: 162 | Fat: 5.1g | Saturated Fat: 1.8g | Carbohydrates: 20.1g | Sugar: 2.1g | Protein: 8.7g

🕐 Prep Time 10 m | 🕐 Cooking Time 35 m | 10 Servings

Ingredients:

- 2/3 cup onion, chopped
- 1 cup cheddar Jack cheese, shredded
- ½ cup Swiss cheese, shredded
- ¼ cup Parmesan cheese, shredded
- 2/3 cup whipped salad dressing
- ½ cup milk
- Salt, to taste

Instructions:

1. In a large bowl, add all the ingredients and mix well.
2. Transfer the mixture into a baking pan. and spread in an even layer.
3. Arrange the "Crisper Basket" in the pot of Ninja Foodi Grill.
4. Close the Ninja Foodi Grill with lid and select "Bake".
5. Set the temperature to 375 degrees F to preheat.
6. Press "Start/Stop" to begin preheating.
7. When the display shows "Add Food" open the lid and place the pan into the "Crisper Basket".
8. Close the Ninja Foodi Grill with lid and set the time for 45 minutes.
9. Press "Start/Stop" to begin cooking.
10. When cooking time is completed, press "Start/Stop" to stop cooking and open the lid.
11. Serve hot.

Nutritional Information per Serving:

Calories: 87 | Fat: 6 g | Saturated Fat: 3.5 g | Carbohydrates: 2.3 g | Sugar: 1.1 g | Protein: 5.1 g

⏰ Prep Time 15 m | ⏰ Cooking Time 25 m | 3 Servings

Ingredients:

- 1 onion, finely chopped
- 1 teaspoon lemon zest, grated
- 1 tablespoon soy sauce
- 1½ tablespoons honey
- Ground white pepper, to taste
- 1 pound chicken wings, rinsed and trimmed
- ½ cup cornstarch

Instructions:

1. In a bowl, mix together the lemongrass, onion, soy sauce, honey, salt, and white pepper.
2. Add the wings and coat with marinade generously.
3. Cover and refrigerate to marinate overnight.
4. Arrange the greased "Crisper Basket" in the pot of Ninja Foodi Grill.
5. Close the Ninja Foodi Grill with lid and select "Air Crisp".
6. Set the temperature to 355 degrees F to preheat.
7. Press "Start/Stop" to begin preheating.
8. Remove the chicken wings from marinade and coat with the cornstarch.
9. When the display shows "Add Food" open the lid and place the chicken wings into the "Crisper Basket" in a single layer.
10. Close the Ninja Foodi Grill with lid and select "Air Crisp".
11. Set the temperature to 360 degrees F for 25 minutes.
12. Press "Start/Stop" to begin cooking.
13. After 13 minutes of cooking, flip the wings once.
14. When the cooking time is completed, press "Start/Stop" to stop cooking and open the lid.
15. serve hot.

Nutritional Information per Serving:
Calories: 418 | Fat: 11.3g | Saturated Fat: 3.1g | Carbohydrates: 32.1g | Sugar: 10.3g | Protein: 44.6g

⏰ Prep Time 20 m | ⏰ Cooking Time 12 m | 4 Servings

Ingredients:

- ½ cup flour
- ¼ teaspoon paprika
- Salt and ground white pepper, to taste
- 2 egg whites

- ¾ cup panko breadcrumbs
- ½ cup unsweetened coconut, shredded
- 2 teaspoons lemon zest, grated finely
- 1 pound prawns, peeled and deveined

Instructions:

1. In a shallow plate, place the flour, paprika, salt and white pepper and mix well.
2. In a second shallow plate, add the egg whites and beat lightly.
3. In a third shallow plate, place the breadcrumbs, coconut and lemon zest and mix well.
4. Coat the prawns with flour mixture, then dip into egg whites and finally coat with the coconut mixture.
5. Place the prawns in the greased baking pan.
6. Arrange the "Crisper Basket" in the pot of Ninja Foodi Grill.
7. Close the Ninja Foodi Grill with lid and select "Bake".
8. Set the temperature to 400 degrees F to preheat.
9. Press "Start/Stop" to begin preheating.
10. When the display shows "Add Food" open the lid and place the pan into the "Crisper Basket".
11. Close the Ninja Foodi Grill with lid and set the time for 12 minutes.
12. Press "Start/Stop" to begin cooking.
13. When the cooking time is completed, press "Start/Stop" to stop cooking and open the lid.
14. Serve hot.

Nutritional Information per Serving:

Calories: 310 | Fat: 6.9g | Saturated Fat: 4.1g | Carbohydrates: 18.7g | Sugar: 0.9g | Protein: 30.2g

⏰ Prep Time 15 m | ⏰ Cooking Time 20 m | 4 Servings

Ingredients:

- 8 ounces coconut milk
- Salt and freshly ground black pepper, to taste
- ½ cup panko breadcrumbs
- ½ teaspoon cayenne pepper
- 1 pound shrimp, peeled and deveined

Instructions:

1. In a shallow dish, mix together the coconut milk, salt and black pepper.
2. In another shallow dish, mix together breadcrumbs, cayenne pepper, salt and black pepper.
3. Dip the shrimp in coconut milk mixture and then coat with the breadcrumbs mixture.
4. Arrange the "Crisper Basket" in the pot of Ninja Foodi Grill.
5. Close the Ninja Foodi Grill with lid and select "Air Crisp".
6. Set the temperature to 350 degrees F to preheat.
7. Press "Start/Stop" to begin preheating.
8. When the display shows "Add Food" open the lid and place the shrimp into the "Crisper Basket".
9. Close the Ninja Foodi Grill with lid and set the time for 20 minutes.
10. Press "Start/Stop" to begin cooking.
11. When the cooking time is completed, press "Start/Stop" to stop cooking and open the lid.
12. Serve warm.

Nutritional Information per Serving:

Calories: 301 | Fat: 15.7g | Saturated Fat: 12.6g | Carbohydrates: 12.5g | Sugar: 2.2g | Protein: 28.2g

⏰ Prep Time 15 m | ⏰ Cooking Time 17 m | 6 Servings

Ingredients:

- 1 pound bacon, thinly sliced
- 1 pound shrimp, peeled and deveined

Instructions:

1. Wrap each shrimp with one bacon slice.
2. Arrange the shrimp in a baking pan and refrigerate for about 20 minutes.
3. Arrange the "Crisper Basket" in the pot of Ninja Foodi Grill.
4. Close the Ninja Foodi Grill with lid and select "Air Crisp".
5. Set the temperature to 390 degrees F to preheat.
6. Press "Start/Stop" to begin preheating.
7. When the display shows "Add Food" open the lid and place the shrimp in the "Crisper Basket" in a single layer.
8. Close the Ninja Foodi Grill with lid and set the time for 7 minutes.
9. Press "Start/Stop" to begin cooking.
10. When cooking time is completed, press "Start/Stop" to stop cooking and open the lid.
11. Serve warm.

Nutritional Information per Serving:

Calories: 499 | Fat: 32.9g | Saturated Fat: 10.8g | Carbohydrates: 2.2g | Sugar: 0g | Protein: 42.5g

⏰ Prep Time 15 m | ⏰ Cooking Time 14 m | 3 Servings

Ingredients:

- ½ pound ground turkey
- 1 onion, chopped
- 1 teaspoon garlic paste
- 2 tablespoons fresh basil, chopped
- 1 teaspoon mustard
- 1 teaspoon maple syrup
- 1 tablespoon Cheddar cheese, grated
- Salt and freshly ground black pepper, to taste

Instructions:

1. In a bowl, add all ingredients and mix until well combined.
2. Make small equal-sized balls from the mixture.
3. Arrange the greased "Crisper Basket" in the pot of Ninja Foodi Grill.
4. Close the Ninja Foodi Grill with lid and select "Air Crisp".
5. Set the temperature to 390 degrees F to preheat.
6. Press "Start/Stop" to begin preheating.
7. When the display shows "Add Food" open the lid and arrange the meatballs in "Crisper Basket".
8. Close the Ninja Foodi Grill with lid and set the time for 14 minutes.
9. Press "Start/Stop" to begin cooking.
10. When cooking time is completed, press "Start/Stop" to stop cooking and open the lid.
11. Serve hot.

Nutritional Information per Serving:

Calories: 184 | Fat: 9.5g | Saturated Fat: 1.9g | Carbohydrates: 5.7g | Sugar: 3g | Protein: 22.1g

🕐 Prep Time 15 m | 🕐 Cooking Time 10 m | 8 Servings

Ingredients:

- 2/3 pound bacon strips
- 14 ounces little smokies
- 1/3 cup brown sugar

Instructions:

1. Cut the bacon strips into thirds across the width.
2. In a shallow dish, place the brown sugar.
3. Coat both sides of bacon strips with brown sugar.
4. Wrap each smokie with a bacon piece.
5. Then secure each wrapped smokie with a toothpick.
6. Arrange the "Crisper Basket" in the pot of Ninja Foodi Grill.
7. Close the Ninja Foodi Grill with lid and select "Air Crisp".
8. Set the temperature to 350 degrees F to preheat.
9. Press "Start/Stop" to begin preheating.
10. When the display shows "Add Food" open the lid and arrange the wrapped smokies in "Crisper Basket" in a single layer.
11. Close the Ninja Foodi Grill with lid and set the time for 10 minutes.
12. Press "Start/Stop" to begin cooking.
13. Flip the smokies once halfway through.
14. When cooking time is completed, press "Start/Stop" to stop cooking and open the lid.
15. Serve warm.

Nutritional Information per Serving:

Calories: 384 | Fat: 30.4g | Saturated Fat: 14.6g | Carbohydrates: 7.3g | Sugar: 6.7g | Protein: 19.2g

⏰ Prep Time 15 m | ⏱ Cooking Time 15 m | 2 Servings

Ingredients:

- ½ pound potatoes, peeled, grated and squeezed
- ½ tablespoon fresh rosemary, chopped finely
- ½ tablespoon fresh thyme, chopped finely

- 1/8 teaspoon red pepper flakes, crushed
- Salt and freshly ground black pepper, to taste
- 2 tablespoons butter, softened

Instructions:

1. In a bowl, mix together the potato, herbs, red pepper flakes, salt and black pepper.
2. Arrange the potato mixture into a lightly greased baking pan and shape it into an even circle.
3. Arrange the "Crisper Basket" in the pot of Ninja Foodi Grill.
4. Close the Ninja Foodi Grill with lid and select "Air Crisp".
5. Set the temperature to 355 degrees F to preheat.
6. Press "Start/Stop" to begin preheating.
7. When the display shows "Add Food" open the lid and place the pan into the "Crisper Basket".
8. Close the Ninja Foodi Grill with lid and set the time for 15 minutes.
9. Press "Start/Stop" to begin cooking.
10. When the cooking time is completed, press "Start/Stop" to stop cooking and open the lid.
11. Cut the potato rosti into wedges.
12. Top with the butter and serve immediately.

Nutritional Information per Serving:

Calories: 185 | Fat: 11.8g | Saturated Fat: 7.4g | Carbohydrates: 18.9g | Sugar: 1.3g | Protein: 2.1g

⏰ Prep Time 15 m | ⏱ Cooking Time 13 m | 6 Servings

Ingredients:

- 12 large jalapeño peppers
- 8 ounces cream cheese, softened
- ¼ cup scallion, chopped
- ¼ cup fresh cilantro, chopped
- ¼ teaspoon onion powder
- ¼ teaspoon garlic powder
- Salt, to taste
- 1/3 cup sharp cheddar cheese, grated

Instructions:

1. Carefully cut off one-third of each pepper lengthwise and then, scoop out the seeds and membranes.
2. In a bowl, mix together the cream cheese, scallion, cilantro, spices and salt.
3. Stuff each pepper with the cream cheese mixture and top with cheese.
4. Arrange the jalapeño peppers into the greased baking pan.
5. Arrange the "Crisper Basket" in the pot of Ninja Foodi Grill.
6. Close the Ninja Foodi Grill with lid and select "Air Crisp".
7. Set the temperature to 400 degrees F to preheat.
8. Press "Start/Stop" to begin preheating.
9. When the display shows "Add Food" open the lid and place the pan into the "Crisper Basket".
10. Close the Ninja Foodi Grill with lid and set the time for 13 minutes.
11. Press "Start/Stop" to begin cooking.
12. When the cooking time is completed, press "Start/Stop" to stop cooking and open the lid.
13. Serve immediately.

Nutritional Information per Serving:

Calories: 171 | Fat: 15.7g | Saturated Fat: 9.7g | Carbohydrates: 3.7g | Sugar: 1.2g | Protein: 4.9g

⏰ Prep Time 15 m | ⏰ Cooking Time 14 m | 8 Servings

Ingredients:

- 3 tablespoons coconut oil
- 1 cup panko breadcrumbs
- ½ cup corn flour
- 2 eggs

- 4 bananas, peeled and halved lengthwise
- 3 tablespoons sugar
- ¼ teaspoon ground cinnamon
- 2 tablespoons walnuts, chopped

Instructions:

1. In a medium skillet, melt the coconut oil over medium heat and cook breadcrumbs for about 3-4 minutes or until golden browned and crumbled, stirring continuously.
2. Transfer the breadcrumbs into a shallow bowl and set aside to cool.
3. In a second bowl, place the corn flour.
4. In a third bowl, whisk the eggs.
5. Coat the banana slices with flour and then, dip into eggs and finally, coat evenly with the breadcrumbs.
6. In a small bowl, mix together the Sugar: and cinnamon.
7. Arrange the "Crisper Basket" in the pot of Ninja Foodi Grill.
8. Close the Ninja Foodi Grill with lid and select "Air Crisp".
9. Set the temperature to 280 degrees F to preheat.
10. Press "Start/Stop" to begin preheating.
11. When the display shows "Add Food" open the lid and place the banana slices into the "Crisper Basket".
12. Sprinkle the banana slices with cinnamon sugar.
13. Close the Ninja Foodi Grill with lid and set the time for 10 minutes.
14. Press "Start/Stop" to begin cooking.
15. When the cooking time is completed, press "Start/Stop" to stop cooking and open the lid.
16. Transfer the banana slices onto serving plates and set aside to cool slightly
17. Sprinkle with chopped walnuts and serve.

Nutritional Information per Serving:

Calories: 216 | Fat: 8.8g | Saturated Fat: 5.3g | Carbohydrates: 26g | Sugar: 11.9g | Protein: 3.4g

⏰ Prep Time 10 m | ⏰ Cooking Time 10 m | 4 Servings

Ingredients:

For Stuffed Apples:

- 4 small firm apples, cored
- ½ cup golden raisins
- ½ cup blanched almonds
- 2 tablespoons sugar

For Vanilla Sauce:

- ½ cup whipped cream
- 2 tablespoons sugar
- ½ teaspoon vanilla extract

Instructions:

1. In a food processor, add the raisins, almonds, and Sugar: and pulse until chopped.
2. Carefully stuff each apple with raisin mixture.
3. Line a baking pan with parchment paper.
4. Place apples into the prepared baking pan.
5. Arrange the "Crisper Basket" in the pot of Ninja Foodi Grill.
6. Close the Ninja Foodi Grill with lid and select "Air Crisp".
7. Set the temperature to 355 degrees F to preheat.
8. Press "Start/Stop" to begin preheating.
9. When the display shows "Add Food" open the lid and place the pan into the "Crisper Basket".
10. Close the Ninja Foodi Grill with lid and set the time for 10 minutes.
11. Press "Start/Stop" to begin cooking.
12. Meanwhile, for vanilla sauce: in a pan, add the cream, sugar, and vanilla extract over medium heat and cook for about 2-3 minutes or until sugar is dissolved, stirring continuously.
13. When the cooking time is completed, press "Start/Stop" to stop cooking and open the lid.
14. Transfer the apples onto the serving plates and set aside to cool slightly
15. Top with the vanilla sauce and serve.

Nutritional Information per Serving:

Calories: 329 | Fat: 11.1g | Saturated Fat: 3.4g | Carbohydrates: 60.2g | Sugar: 46.5g | Protein: 4g

🕐 Prep Time 10 m | 🕐 Cooking Time 30 m | 2 Servings

Ingredients:

- 1 ripe Anjou pear, halved and cored
- 1/8 teaspoon ground cinnamon
- 6 semisweet chocolate chips

- 2 tablespoons pecans, chopped
- 1 teaspoon pure maple syrup

Instructions:

1. Arrange the pear halves onto the greased baking pan cut sides up and sprinkle with cinnamon.
2. Top each half with chocolate chips and pecans and drizzle with maple syrup.
3. Arrange the "Crisper Basket" in the pot of Ninja Foodi Grill.
4. Close the Ninja Foodi Grill with lid and select "Air Crisp".
5. Set the temperature to 350 degrees F to preheat.
6. Press "Start/Stop" to begin preheating.
7. When the display shows "Add Food" open the lid and place the pan into the "Crisper Basket".
8. Close the Ninja Foodi Grill with lid and set the time for 30 minutes.
9. Press "Start/Stop" to begin cooking.
10. When the cooking time is completed, press "Start/Stop" to stop cooking and open the lid.
11. Serve warm.

Nutritional Information per Serving:

Calories: 111 | Fat: 6 g | Saturated Fat: 0.9 g | Carbohydrates: 15 g | Sugar: 9.9 g | Protein: 1.2 g

🕐 Prep Time 15 m | 🕐 Cooking Time 5 m | 2 Servings

Ingredients:

- 4 tablespoons strawberry jelly
- 2 soft shell tortillas
- ¼ cup fresh blueberries
- ¼ cup fresh raspberries
- 2 tablespoons powdered sugar

Instructions:

1. Spread 2 tablespoons of strawberry jelly over each tortilla
2. Top each with berries evenly and sprinkle with powdered sugar.
3. Arrange the "Crisper Basket" in the pot of Ninja Foodi Grill.
4. Close the Ninja Foodi Grill with lid and select "Air Crisp".
5. Set the temperature to 300 degrees F to preheat.
6. Press "Start/Stop" to begin preheating.
7. When the display shows "Add Food" open the lid and place the tortillas into the "Crisper Basket".
8. Close the Ninja Foodi Grill with lid and set the time for 5 minutes.
9. Press "Start/Stop" to begin cooking.
10. When the cooking time is completed, press "Start/Stop" to stop cooking and open the lid.
11. Serve warm.

Nutritional Information per Serving:

Calories: 202 | Fat: 0.9g | Saturated Fat: 0.1g | Carbohydrates: 49.2g | Sugar: 34.5g | Protein: 1.7g

⏰ Prep Time 15 m | ⏰ Cooking Time 6 m | 8 Servings

Ingredients:

- 2 cups powdered sugar
- ¼ cup whole milk
- 1 teaspoon vanilla extract

- 1 (16-ounce) tube prepared biscuit dough
- Olive oil cooking spray
- ½ teaspoon ground cinnamon

Instructions:

1. For glaze: in a medium bowl, place the powdered sugar, milk and vanilla extract and beat well. Set aside.
2. Arrange the biscuit dough onto a smooth surface.
3. With a 1-inch ring mold, cut a hole in the center of each round of dough.
4. Place dough rounds onto a plate and refrigerate for about 5 minutes.
5. Coat each dough round with cooking spray evenly.
6. Arrange the "Grill Grate" in the pot of Ninja Foodi Grill.
7. Close the Ninja Foodi Grill with lid and select "Grill".
8. Set the temperature to "Medium" to preheat.
9. Press "Start/Stop" to begin preheating.
10. When the display shows "Add Food" open the lid and place 4 donut rounds onto the "Grill Grate".
11. Close the Ninja Foodi Grill with lid and set the time for 3 minutes.
12. Press "Start/Stop" to begin cooking.
13. When the cooking time is completed, press "Start/Stop" to stop cooking and open the lid.
14. Transfer the donuts onto a platter.
15. Repeat with the remaining donuts.
16. Sprinkle the warm donuts with cinnamon and serve immediately.

Nutritional Information per Serving:

Calories: 389 | Fat: 17.7g | Saturated Fat: 4.5g | Carbohydrates: 54.4g | Sugar: 29.9g | Protein: 3.5g

⏰ Prep Time 10 m | ⏰ Cooking Time 30 m | 1 Cake

Ingredients:

- ¼ cup all-purpose flour
- ¼ teaspoon baking soda
- 1/8 teaspoon ground cinnamon
- 1/8 teaspoon salt
- ½ cup banana, peeled and mashed

- 2 tablespoons sugar
- 1 tablespoon butter, melted
- 1 egg yolk
- ¼ teaspoon vanilla extract

Instructions:

1. In a bowl, mix together the flour, baking soda, cinnamon and salt.
2. In another bowl, add the mashed banana and sugar and beat well.
3. Add the butter, the egg yolk, and the vanilla and mix well.
4. Add the flour mixture and mix until just combined.
5. Place the mixture into a lightly greased ramekin.
6. Arrange the "Crisper Basket" in the pot of Ninja Foodi Grill.
7. Close the Ninja Foodi Grill with lid and select "Bake".
8. Set the temperature to 350 degrees F to preheat.
9. Press "Start/Stop" to begin preheating.
10. When the display shows "Add Food" open the lid and place the ramekin into the "Crisper Basket".
11. Close the Ninja Foodi Grill with lid and set the time for 30 minutes.
12. Press "Start/Stop" to begin cooking.
13. When the cooking time is completed, press "Start/Stop" to stop cooking and open the lid.
14. Place the ramekin onto a wire rack to cool slightly before serving.

Nutritional Information per Serving:

Calories: 430 | Fat: 16.6g | Saturated Fat: 9g | Carbohydrates: 66g | Sugar: 33.5g | Protein: 6.9g

⏰ Prep Time 20 m | ⏰ Cooking Time 12 m | 12 Servings

Ingredients:

For Cupcakes

- 2 cups refined flour
- ¾ cup icing sugar
- 2 teaspoons beet powder
- 1 teaspoon cocoa powder
- ¾ cup peanut butter
- 3 eggs

For Frosting

- 1 cup butter
- 1 (8-ounce) package cream cheese, softened
- 2 teaspoons vanilla extract
- ¼ teaspoon salt
- 4½ cups powdered sugar

For Garnishing

- ½ cup fresh raspberries

Instructions:

1. For cupcakes: in a bowl, add all the ingredients and with an electric whisker, whisk until well combined.
2. Place the mixture into silicon cups.
3. Arrange the "Crisper Basket" in the pot of Ninja Foodi Grill.
4. Close the Ninja Foodi Grill with lid and select "Air Crisp".
5. Set the temperature to 340 degrees F to preheat.
6. Press "Start/Stop" to begin preheating.
7. When the display shows "Add Food" open the lid and place the silicon cups into the "Crisper Basket".
8. Close the Ninja Foodi Grill with lid and set the time for 12 minutes.
9. Press "Start/Stop" to begin cooking.
10. When the cooking time is completed, press "Start/Stop" to stop cooking and open the lid.
11. Place the silicon cups onto a wire rack to cool for about 10 minutes.
12. Carefully invert the cupcakes onto the wire rack to completely cool before frosting.
13. For frosting: in a large bowl, mix well butter, cream cheese, vanilla extract, and salt.
14. Add the powdered sugar, one cup at a time, whisking well after each addition.
15. Spread frosting evenly over each cupcake.
16. Garnish with raspberries and serve.

Nutritional Information per Serving:

Calories: 599 | Fat: 31.5g | Saturated Fat: 16g | Carbohydrates: 73.2g | Sugar: 53.4g | Protein: 9.3g

⏰ Prep Time 15 m | ⏱ Cooking Time 15 m | 12 Servings

Ingredients:

- 1 1/3 cups self-rising flour
- 2/3 cup plus 3 tablespoons caster Sugar:
- 2½ tablespoons cocoa powder
- 3½ ounces butter
- 5 tablespoons milk

- 2 medium eggs
- ½ teaspoon vanilla extract
- Water, as needed
- ½ ounces milk chocolate, finely chopped

Instructions:

1. In a bowl, mix well flour, sugar, and cocoa powder.
2. With a pastry cutter, cut in the butter until a breadcrumb-like mixture forms.
3. In another bowl, mix together the milk and eggs.
4. Add the egg mixture into flour mixture and mix until well combined.
5. Add the vanilla extract and a little water and mix until well combined.
6. Fold in the chopped chocolate.
7. Grease 12 muffin moulds.
8. Transfer mixture into the prepared muffin molds evenly.
9. Arrange the "Crisper Basket" in the pot of Ninja Foodi Grill.
10. Close the Ninja Foodi Grill with lid and select "Air Crisp".
11. Set the temperature to 355 degrees F to preheat.
12. Press "Start/Stop" to begin preheating.
13. When the display shows "Add Food" open the lid and place the muffin molds into the "Crisper Basket".
14. Close the Ninja Foodi Grill with lid and set the time for 9 minutes.
15. Press "Start/Stop" to begin cooking.
16. After 9 minutes of cooking, set the temperature to 320 degrees F for 6 minutes.
17. When the cooking time is completed, press "Start/Stop" to stop cooking and open the lid.
18. Place the muffin molds onto a wire rack to cool for about 10 minutes.
19. Now, invert the muffins onto the wire rack to cool completely before serving.

Nutritional Information per Serving:

Calories: 389 | Fat: 31.2g | Saturated Fat: 19.5g | Carbohydrates: 26.3g | Sugar: 15.1g | Protein: 3.2g

CPSIA information can be obtained
at www.ICGtesting.com
Printed in the USA
LVHW062013190121
676877LV00007B/345